ICE Conditions of Contract

Seventh Edition

CONDITIONS OF CONTRACT AND FORMS OF TENDER, AGREEMENT AND BOND FOR USE IN CONNECTION WITH WORKS OF CIVIL ENGINEERING CONSTRUCTION

Measurement Version

The Institution of Civil Engineers
The Association of Consulting Engineers
The Civil Engineering Contractors Association

Published by Thomas Telford Publishing, Thomas Telford Limited, 1 Heron Quay,London E14 4JD on behalf of:

The Chief Executive and Secretary
The Institution of Civil Engineers
One Great George Street
London SW1P 3AA

The Chief Executive
The Association of Consulting Engineers
Alliance House
12 Caxton Street
London SW1H 0QL

The Director
The Civil Engineering Contractors Association
Construction House
56-64 Leonard Street
London   EC2A 4JX

First edition was agreed by The Institution of Civil Engineers and The Federation of Civil Engineering Contractors, December 1945
Second to Sixth editions were approved by The Institution of Civil Engineers, The
          Association of Consulting Engineers and The Federation of Civil Engineering Contractors
Second edition, January 1950
Third edition, March 1951
Fourth edition, January 1955
Fifth edition, June 1973; revised January 1979; reprinted with amendments January 1986
Sixth edition, January 1991;   reprinted with amendments November 1995;
                                reprinted with amendments November 1997
Seventh edition was approved by The Institution of Civil Engineers, The Association of Consulting Engineers and The Civil Engineering Contractors Association, September 1999.

The Institution of Civil Engineers, The Association of Consulting Engineers and The Civil Engineering Contractors Association have, as sponsoring authorities, approved this revised, seventh, edition of the document commonly known as the ICE Conditions of Contract, for all works of civil engineering construction. A permanent joint committee has prepared and will keep under review the use of the document and will consider any suggestions for amendment, which should be addressed to the Chief Executive and Secretary (CCSJC), The Institution of Civil Engineers, One Great George Street, London SW1P 3AA. Revision to the document will be made when such action seems warranted.

9 8 7 6 5 4 3 2 1

ISBN 0 7277 2789 3

A catalogue record for this book is available from the British Library

Printed and bound in Great Britain by Selwood Printing, West Sussex

CONTENTS

Associated publications referred to in the Contract

Guidance Notes to the ICE Conditions of Contract 7th Edition

ICE Arbitration Procedure 1997
ICE Arbitration Procedure (Scotland) (1983)
ICE Conciliation Procedure 1999
ICE Adjudication Procedure 1997

Other ICE Conditions of Contract publications
ICE Design and Construct Conditions of Contract
Guidance Notes to the ICE Design and Construct Conditions of Contract
ICE Conditions of Contract for Minor Works 2nd edition (including Guidance Notes)

CONTENTS OF THE ICE CONDITIONS OF CONTRACT

MATERIALS AND WORKMANSHIP

COMMENCEMENT TIME AND DELAYS

LIQUIDATED DAMAGES FOR DELAY

CERTIFICATE OF SUBSTANTIAL COMPLETION

OUTSTANDING WORK AND DEFECTS

ALTERATIONS ADDITIONS AND OMISSIONS

PROPERTY IN MATERIALS AND CONTRACTOR'S EQUIPMENT

MEASUREMENT

PROVISIONAL AND PRIME COST SUMS AND NOMINATED SUB-CONTRACTS

CERTIFICATES AND PAYMENT

REMEDIES AND POWERS

AVOIDANCE AND SETTLEMENT OF DISPUTES

APPLICATION TO SCOTLAND AND NORTHERN IRELAND

NOTICES

TAX MATTERS

THE CONSTRUCTION (DESIGN AND MANAGEMENT) REGULATIONS 1994

SPECIAL CONDITIONS

INDEX

ICE Conditions of Contract - Measurement Version

DEFINITIONS AND INTERPRETATION

Definitions   **1**   (1) In the Contract (as hereinafter defined) the following words and expressions shall have the meanings hereby assigned to them except where the context otherwise requires.

    (a)   "Employer" means the person or persons firm company or other body named in the Appendix to the Form of Tender and includes the Employer's personal representatives successors and permitted assignees.

    (b)   "Contractor" means the person or persons firm or company to whom the Contract has been awarded by the Employer and includes the Contractor's personal representatives successors and permitted assignees.

    (c)   "Engineer" means the person firm or company appointed by the Employer to act as Engineer for the purposes of the Contract and named in the Appendix to the Form of Tender or any other person firm or company so appointed from time to time by the Employer and notified in writing as such to the Contractor.

    (d)   "Engineer's Representative" means a person notified as such from time to time by the Engineer under Clause 2(3)(a).

    (e)   "Contract" means the Conditions of Contract Specification Drawings Bill of Quantities the Form of Tender the written acceptance thereof and the Form of Agreement (if completed).

    (f)   "Specification" means the specification referred to in the Form of Tender and any modification thereof or addition thereto as may from time to time be furnished or approved in writing by the Engineer.

    (g)   "Drawings" means the drawings referred to in the Specification and any modification of such drawings approved in writing by the Engineer and such other drawings as may from time to time be furnished by or approved in writing by the Engineer.

    (h)   "Bill of Quantities" means the priced and completed Bill of Quantities.

    (i)   "Tender Total" means the total of the Bill of Quantities at the date of award of the Contract or in the absence of a Bill of Quantities the agreed estimated total value of the Works at that date.

    (j)   "Contract Price" means the sum to be ascertained and paid in accordance with the provisions hereinafter contained for the construction and completion of the Works in accordance with the Contract.

(k)   "Prime Cost (PC) Item" means an item in the Contract which contains (either wholly or in part) a sum referred to as Prime Cost (PC) which will be used for the carrying out of work or the supply of goods materials or services for the Works.

(l)   "Provisional Sum" means a sum included and so designated in the Contract as a specific contingency for the carrying out of work or the supply of goods materials or services which may be used in whole or in part or not at all at the direction and discretion of the Engineer.

(m)   "Nominated Sub-contractor" means any merchant tradesman specialist or other person firm or company nominated in accordance with the Contract to be employed by the Contractor for the carrying out of work or supply of goods materials or services for which a Prime Cost or a Provisional Sum has been included in the Contract.

(n)   "Permanent Works" means the permanent works to be constructed and completed in accordance with the Contract.

(o)   "Temporary Works" means all temporary works of every kind required in or about the construction and completion of the Works.

(p)   "Works" means the Permanent Works together with the Temporary Works.

(q)   "Works Commencement Date"—as defined in Clause 41 (1).

(r)   "Certificate of Substantial Completion" means a certificate issued under Clause 48.

(s)   "Defects Correction Period" means that period stated in the Appendix to the Form of Tender calculated from the date on which the Contractor becomes entitled to a Certificate of Substantial Completion for the Works or any Section or part thereof.

(t)   "Defects Correction Certificate"—as defined in Clause 61 (1).

(u)   "Section" means a part of the Works separately identified in the Appendix to the Form of Tender.

(v)   "Site" means the lands and other places on under in or through which the Works are to be constructed and any other lands or places provided by the Employer for the purposes of the Contract together with such other places as may be designated in the Contract or subsequently agreed by the Engineer as forming part of the Site.

(w)   "Contractor's Equipment" means all appliances or things of whatsoever nature required in or about the construction and completion of the Works but does not include materials or other things intended to form or forming part of the Permanent Works.

Singular and plural

(2)   Words importing the singular also include the plural and vice-versa where the context requires.

Ieadings and marginal notes

(3)   The headings and marginal notes in the Conditions of Contract shall not be deemed to be part thereof or be taken into consideration in the interpretation or construction thereof or of the Contract.

Clause references

(4)   All references herein to clauses are references to clauses numbered in the Conditions of Contract and not to those in any other document forming part of the Contract.

Cost

(5)   The word "cost" when used in the Conditions of Contract means all expenditure properly incurred or to be incurred whether on or off the Site including overhead finance and other charges properly allocatable thereto but does not include any allowance for profit.

Communications in writing

(6)   Communications which under the Contract are required to be "in writing" may be hand-written typewritten or printed and sent by hand post telex cable facsimile or other means resulting in a permanent record.

ENGINEER AND ENGINEER'S REPRESENTATIVE

Duties and authority of Engineer   2

(1)   (a)   The Engineer shall carry out the duties specified in or necessarily to be implied from the Contract.

(b)   The Engineer may exercise the authority specified in or necessarily to be implied from the Contract. If the Engineer is required under the terms of his appointment by the Employer to obtain the specific approval of the Employer before exercising any such authority particulars of such requirements shall be those set out in the Appendix to the Form of Tender. Any requisite approval shall be deemed to have been given by the Employer for any such authority exercised by the Engineer.

(c)   Except as expressly stated in the Contract the Engineer shall have no authority to amend the Contract nor to relieve the Contractor of any of his obligations under the Contract.

(d)   The giving of any consent or approval by or on behalf of the Engineer shall not in any way relieve the Contractor of any of his obligations under the Contract or of his duty to ensure the correctness or accuracy of the matter or thing which is the subject of the consent or approval.

Named individual

(2)   (a)   Where the Engineer as defined in Clause 1 (1)(c) is not a single named Chartered Engineer the Engineer shall within 7 days of the award of the Contract and in any event before the Works Commencement Date notify to the Contractor in writing the name of the Chartered Engineer who will act on his behalf and assume the full responsibilities of the Engineer under the Contract.

(b)   The Engineer shall thereafter in like manner notify the Contractor of any replacement of the named Chartered Engineer.

**Engineer's
Representative**

(3) (a) The Engineer's Representative shall be responsible to the Engineer who shall notify his appointment to the Contractor in writing.

(b) The Engineer's Representative shall watch and supervise the construction and completion of the Works. He shall have no authority

(i) to relieve the Contractor of any of his duties or obligations under the Contract

nor except as expressly provided for in sub-clause (4) of this Clause

(ii) to order any work involving delay or any extra payment by the Employer or

(iii) to make any variation of or in the Works.

Delegation by Engineer

(4) The Engineer may from time to time delegate to the Engineer's Representative or any other person responsible to the Engineer any of the duties and authorities vested in the Engineer and he may at any time revoke such delegation. Any such delegation

(a) shall be in writing and shall not take effect until such time as a copy thereof has been delivered to the Contractor or his agent appointed under Clause 15(2)

(b) shall continue in force until such time as the Engineer shall notify the Contractor in writing that the same has been revoked

(c) shall not be given in respect of any decision to be taken or certificate to be issued under Clauses 12(6) 44 46(3) 48 60(4) 61 65 or 66.

Assistants

(5) (a) The Engineer or the Engineer's Representative may appoint any number of persons to assist the Engineer's Representative in the carrying out of his duties under sub-clause (3)(b) or (4) of this Clause. He shall notify to the Contractor the names duties and scope of authority of such persons.

(b) Such assistants shall have no authority to issue any instructions to the Contractor save insofar as such instructions may be necessary to enable them to carry out their duties and to secure the acceptance of materials and workmanship as being in accordance with the Contract. Any instructions given by an assistant for these purposes shall where appropriate be in writing and be deemed to have been given by the Engineer's Representative.

(c) If the Contractor is dissatisfied by reason of any instruction of any assistant of the Engineer's Representative appointed under sub-clause (5)(a) of this Clause he shall be entitled to refer the matter to the Engineer's Representative who shall thereupon confirm reverse or vary such instruction.

Instructions

(6) (a) Instructions given by the Engineer or by any person exercising delegated duties and authorities under sub-clause (4) of this Clause shall be in writing. Provided that if for any reason it is considered necessary to give any such instruction orally the Contractor shall comply therewith.

(b) Any such oral instruction shall be confirmed in writing as soon as is possible under the circumstances. Provided that if the Contractor confirms in writing any such oral instruction which confirmation is not contradicted in writing by the Engineer or the Engineer's Representative forthwith it shall be deemed to be an instruction in writing by the Engineer.

(c) Upon the written request of the Contractor the Engineer or the person exercising delegated duties or authorities under sub-clause (4) of this Clause shall specify in writing under which of his duties and authorities the instruction is given.

Impartiality

(7) The Engineer shall act impartially within the terms of the Contract having regard to all the circumstances. In like manner the Engineer's Representative and any person exercising delegated duties and authorities shall also act impartially.

ASSIGNMENT AND SUB-CONTRACTING

Assignment 3

(1) Neither the Employer nor the Contractor shall assign the Contract or any part thereof or any benefit or interest therein or thereunder without the prior written consent of the other party which consent shall not unreasonably be withheld.

(2) Nothing in this Contract confers or purports to confer on any third party any benefit or any right to enforce any term of the Contract.

Sub-contracting 4

(1) The Contractor shall not sub-contract the whole of the Works without the prior written consent of the Employer.

(2) Except where otherwise provided in the Appendix to the Form of Tender the Contractor may sub-contract any part of the Works or their design. The extent of the work to be sub-contracted and the name and address of the sub-contractor must be notified in writing to the Engineer as soon as practicable and in any event not later than 14 days prior to the sub-contractor's entry on to the Site or in the case of design on appointment.

Provided that if not later than 7 days after receipt of such notification the Engineer for good reason objects to the Contractor in writing the sub-contractor so notified shall not be employed on or in connection with the Works. Such objection must be accompanied by reasons in writing.

(3) The employment of labour-only sub-contractors does not require notification to the Engineer under sub-clause (2) of this Clause.

(4) The Contractor shall be and remain liable under the Contract for all work sub-contracted by him and for acts defaults or neglects of any sub-contractor his agents servants or workpeople.

(5) The Engineer shall be at liberty after due warning in writing to require the Contractor to remove from the Works or their design any sub-contractor who mis-conducts himself or is incompetent or negligent in the performance of his duties or fails to conform with any particular provisions with regard to safety which may be set out in the Contract or persists in any conduct which is prejudicial to safety or health and such sub-contractor shall not be again employed upon the Works without the permission of the Engineer.

CONTRACT DOCUMENTS

Documents mutually explanatory   **5**   The several documents forming the Contract are to be taken as mutually explanatory of one another and in case of ambiguities or discrepancies the same shall be explained and adjusted by the Engineer who shall thereupon issue to the Contractor appropriate instructions in writing which shall be regarded as instructions issued in accordance with Clause 13.

Supply of documents   **6**   (1) Upon award of the Contract the following shall be furnished to the Contractor free of charge

     (a) four copies of the Conditions of Contract Specification and (unpriced) bill of quantities and

     (b) the number and type of copies as entered in the Appendix to the Form of Tender of all Drawings listed in the Specification.

(2) Upon approval by the Engineer in accordance with Clause 7(6) the Contractor shall supply to the Engineer four copies of all Drawings Specifications and other documents submitted by the Contractor. In addition the Contractor shall supply at the Employer's expense such further copies of such Drawings Specifications and other documents as the Engineer may request in writing for his use.

(3) Copyright of all Drawings Specifications and the Bill of Quantities (except the pricing thereof) supplied by the Employer or the Engineer shall not pass to the Contractor but the Contractor may obtain or make at his own expense any further copies required by him for the purposes of the Contract. Similarly copyright in all documents supplied by the Contractor under Clause 7(6) shall remain with the Contractor but the Employer and the Engineer shall have full power to reproduce and use the same for the purpose of completing operating maintaining and adjusting the Works.

Further Drawings Specifications and instructions   **7**   (1) The Engineer shall from time to time during the progress of the Works supply to the Contractor such modified or further Drawings Specifications and instructions as shall in the Engineer's opinion be necessary for the purpose of the proper and adequate construction and completion of the Works and the Contractor shall carry out and be bound by the same.

If such Drawings Specifications or instructions require any variation to any part of the Works the same shall be deemed to have been issued pursuant to Clause 51.

Contractor to provide further documents   (2) Where sub-clause (6) of this Clause applies the Engineer may require the Contractor to supply such further documents as shall in the Engineer's opinion be necessary for the purpose of the proper and adequate construction completion and maintenance of the Works and when accepted by the Engineer the Contractor shall be bound by the same.

Notice by Contractor   (3) The Contractor shall give adequate notice in writing to the Engineer of any further Drawing or Specification that the Contractor may require for the construction and completion of the Works or otherwise under the Contract.

Delay in issue

(4) (a)   If by reason of any failure or inability of the Engineer to issue at a time reasonable in all the circumstances Drawings Specifications or instructions requested by the Contractor and considered necessary by the Engineer in accordance with sub-clause (1) of this Clause the Contractor suffers delay or incurs additional cost then the Engineer shall take such delay into account in determining any extension of time to which the Contractor is entitled under Clause 44 and the Contractor shall subject to Clause 53 be paid in accordance with Clause 60 the amount of such cost as may be reasonable.

(b)   If the failure of the Engineer to issue any Drawing Specification or instruction is caused in whole or in part by the failure of the Contractor after due notice in writing to submit drawings specifications or other documents which he is required to submit under the Contract the Engineer shall take into account such failure by the Contractor in taking any action under sub-clause (4)(a) of this Clause.

One copy of documents to be kept on Site

(5)   One copy of the Drawings and Specification furnished to the Contractor as aforesaid and of all Drawings Specifications and other documents required to be provided by the Contractor under sub-clause (6) of this Clause shall at all reasonable times be available on the Site for inspection and use by the Engineer and the Engineer's Representative and by any other person authorized by the Engineer in writing.

Permanent Works designed by Contractor

(6)   Where the Contract expressly provides that part of the Permanent Works shall be designed by the Contractor he shall submit to the Engineer for acceptance

(a)   such drawings specifications calculations and other information as shall be necessary to satisfy the Engineer that the Contractor's design generally complies with the requirements of the Contract and

(b)   operation and maintenance manuals together with as completed drawings of that part of the Permanent Works in sufficient detail to enable the Employer to operate maintain dismantle reassemble and adjust the Permanent Works incorporating that design. No certificate under Clause 48 covering any part of the Permanent Works designed by the Contractor shall be issued until manuals and drawings in such detail have been submitted to and accepted by the Engineer.

Responsibility unaffected by approval

(7)   Acceptance by the Engineer in accordance with sub-clause (6) of this Clause shall not relieve the Contractor of any of his responsibilities under the Contract. The Engineer shall be responsible for the integration and co-ordination of the Contractor's design with the rest of the Works.

GENERAL OBLIGATIONS

Contractor's general responsibilities   **8**

(1)   The Contractor shall subject to the provisions of the Contract

(a)   construct and complete the Works and

(b)   provide all labour materials Contractor's Equipment Temporary Works transport to and from and in or about the Site and everything whether of a temporary or permanent nature required in and for such construction and completion so far as the necessity for providing the same is specified in or reasonably to be inferred from the Contract.

Design responsibility

(2)   The Contractor shall not be responsible for the design or specification of the Permanent Works or any part thereof (except as may be expressly provided in the Contract) or of any Temporary Works design supplied by the Engineer. The Contractor shall exercise all reasonable skill care and diligence in designing any part of the Permanent Works for which he is responsible.

Contractor responsible for safety of site operations

(3)   The Contractor shall take full responsibility for the adequacy stability and safety of all site operations and methods of construction.

Form of Agreement   9

The Contractor shall if called upon so to do enter into and execute an agreement to be prepared at the cost of the Employer in the form annexed to these Conditions.

Performance security   10

(1)   If the Contract requires the Contractor to provide security for the proper performance of the Contract he shall obtain and provide to the Employer such security in a sum not exceeding 10% of the Tender Total within 28 days of the award of the Contract. The security shall be provided by a body approved by the Employer and be in the Form of Bond annexed to these Conditions. The Contractor shall pay the cost of the security unless the Contract provides otherwise.

Dispute resolution upon security

(2)   For the purposes of the dispute resolution provisions in such security

(a)   the Employer shall be deemed to be a party to the security for the purpose of doing everything necessary to give effect to such provisions and

(b)   any agreement decision award or other determination touching or concerning the relevant date for the discharge of the security shall be wholly without prejudice to the resolution or determination of any dispute between the Employer and the Contractor under Clause 66.

Provision and interpretation of information   11

(1)   As between the Employer and the Contractor and without prejudice to sub-clause (2) of this Clause information on

(a)   the nature of the ground and subsoil and hydrological conditions and

(b)   pipes and cables in on or over the ground

obtained by or on behalf of the Employer from investigations undertaken relevant to the Works shall only be taken into account to the extent that it was made available to the Contractor before the submission of his tender.

The Contractor shall be responsible for the interpretation of all such information for the purposes of constructing the Works and for any design which is the Contractor's responsibility under the Contract.

Inspection of Site

(2)   The Contractor shall be deemed to have inspected and examined the Site and its surroundings and information available in connection therewith and to have satisfied himself so far as is practicable and reasonable before submitting his tender as to

    (a)   the form and nature thereof including the ground and sub-soil and hydrological conditions and

    (b)   the extent and nature of work and materials necessary for constructing and completing the Works and

    (c)   the means of communication with and access to the Site and the accommodation he may require

and in general to have obtained for himself all necessary information as to risks contingencies and all other circumstances which may influence or affect his tender.

Basis and sufficiency of tender

(3)   The Contractor shall be deemed to have

    (a)   based his tender on his own inspection and examination as aforesaid and on all information whether obtainable by him or made available by the Employer and

    (b)   satisfied himself before submitting his tender as to the correctness and sufficiency of the rates and prices stated by him in the Bill of Quantities which shall (unless otherwise provided in the Contract) cover all his obligations under the Contract.

Adverse physical conditions and artificial obstructions

12   (1)   If during the carrying out of the Works the Contractor encounters physical conditions (other than weather conditions or conditions due to weather conditions) or artificial obstructions which conditions or obstructions could not in his opinion reasonably have been foreseen by an experienced contractor the Contractor shall as early as practicable give written notice thereof to the Engineer.

Intention to claim

(2)   If in addition the Contractor intends to make any claim for additional payment or extension of time arising from any such condition or obstruction he shall at the same time or as soon thereafter as may be reasonable inform the Engineer in writing pursuant to Clause 53 and/or Clause 44(1) as may be appropriate specifying the condition or obstruction to which the claim relates.

Measures being taken

(3)   When giving notification or information in accordance with sub-clauses (1) and/or (2) of this Clause or as soon as practicable thereafter the Contractor shall give details of any anticipated effects of the condition or obstruction the measures he has taken is taking or is proposing to take their estimated cost and the extent of the anticipated delay in or interference with the carrying out of the Works.

Action by Engineer

(4)   Following receipt of any notification under sub-clauses (1) or (2) or receipt of details in accordance with sub-clause (3) of this Clause the Engineer may if he thinks fit among other things

(a)   require the Contractor to investigate and report upon the practicality cost and timing of alternative measures which may be available

(b)   give written consent to measures notified under sub-clause (3) of this Clause with or without modification

(c)   give written instructions as to how the physical conditions or artificial obstructions are to be dealt with

(d)   order a suspension under Clause 40 or a variation under Clause 51.

Conditions reasonably foreseeable

(5)   If the Engineer shall decide that the physical conditions or artificial obstructions could in whole or in part have been reasonably foreseen by an experienced contractor he shall so inform the Contractor in writing as soon as he shall have reached that decision but the value of any variation previously ordered by him pursuant to sub-clause (4)(d) of this Clause shall be ascertained in accordance with Clause 52 and included in the Contract Price.

Delay and extra cost

(6)   Where an extension of time or additional payment is claimed pursuant to sub-clause (2) of this Clause the Engineer shall if in his opinion such conditions or obstructions could not reasonably have been foreseen by an experienced contractor

(a)   determine any delay which the Contractor has suffered and

(b)   determine the amount of any costs which may reasonably have been incurred by the Contractor (together with a reasonable percentage addition thereto in respect of profit)

by reason of such conditions or obstructions and shall notify the Contractor accordingly with a copy to the Employer.

Any delay so determined shall forthwith be considered under Clause 44(3) for an appropriate extension of time and the Contractor shall subject to Clause 53 be paid in accordance with Clause 60 the amount so determined.

Work to be to satisfaction of Engineer   13

(1)   Save insofar as it is legally or physically impossible the Contractor shall construct and complete the Works in strict accordance with the Contract to the satisfaction of the Engineer and shall comply with and adhere strictly to the Engineer's instructions on any matter connected therewith (whether mentioned in the Contract or not).   The Contractor shall take instructions only from the Engineer or subject to Clause 2(4) from his duly appointed delegate.

Mode and manner of construction

(2)   The whole of the materials Contractor's Equipment and labour to be provided by the Contractor under Clause 8 and the mode manner and speed of construction of the Works are to be of a kind and conducted in a manner acceptable to the Engineer.

Delay and extra cost

(3)   If in pursuance of Clause 5 or sub-clause (1) of this Clause the Engineer shall issue instructions which involve the Contractor in delay or disrupt his arrangements or methods of construction so as to cause him to incur cost beyond that reasonably to have been foreseen by an experienced contractor at the time of tender then the Engineer shall take such delay into account in determining any extension of time to which the Contractor is entitled under Clause 44 and the Contractor shall subject to Clause 53 be paid in accordance with Clause 60 the amount of such cost as may be reasonable except to the extent that such delay and extra cost result from the Contractor's default.   Profit shall be added thereto in respect of any additional permanent or temporary work.   If such instructions require any variation to any part of the Works the same shall be deemed to have been given pursuant to Clause 51.

Programme to be furnished

14   (1)   (a)   Within 21 days after the award of the Contract the Contractor shall submit to the Engineer for his acceptance a programme showing the order in which he proposes to carry out the Works having regard to the provisions of Clause 42(1) .

(b)   At the same time the Contractor shall also provide in writing for the information of the Engineer a general description of the arrangements and methods of construction which the Contractor proposes to adopt for the carrying out of the Works.

(c)   Should the Engineer reject any programme under sub-clause (2)(b) of this Clause the Contractor shall within 21 days of such rejection submit a revised programme.

Action by Engineer

(2)   The Engineer shall within 21 days after receipt of the Contractor's programme

(a)   accept the programme in writing or

(b)   reject the programme in writing with reasons or

(c)   request the Contractor to supply further information to clarify or substantiate the programme or to satisfy the Engineer as to its reasonableness having regard to the Contractor's obligations under the Contract.

Provided that if none of the above actions is taken within the said period of 21 days the Engineer shall be deemed to have accepted the programme as submitted.

Provision of further information

(3)   The Contractor shall within 21 days after receiving from the Engineer any request under sub-clause (2)(c) of this Clause or within such further period as the Engineer may allow provide the further information requested failing which the relevant programme shall be deemed to be rejected.

Upon receipt of such further information the Engineer shall within a further 21 days accept or reject the programme in accordance with sub-clauses (2)(a) or (2)(b) of this Clause.

Revision of programme

(4)   Should it appear to the Engineer at any time that the actual progress of the work does not conform with the accepted programme referred to in sub-clause (1) of this Clause the Engineer shall be entitled to require the Contractor to produce a revised programme showing such modifications to the original programme as may be necessary to ensure completion of the Works or any Section within the time for completion as defined in Clause 43 or extended time granted pursuant to Clause 44. In such event the Contractor shall submit his revised programme within 21 days or within such further period as the Engineer may allow. Thereafter the provisions of sub-clauses (2) and (3) of this Clause shall apply.

Design criteria

(5)   The Engineer shall provide to the Contractor such design criteria relevant to the Permanent Works or any Temporary Works design supplied by the Engineer as may be necessary to enable the Contractor to comply with sub-clauses (6) and (7) of this Clause.

Methods of construction

(6)   If requested by the Engineer the Contractor shall submit at such times and in such further detail as the Engineer may reasonably require information pertaining to the methods of construction (including Temporary Works and the use of Contractor's Equipment) which the Contractor proposes to adopt or use and calculations of stresses strains and deflections that will arise in the Permanent Works or any parts thereof during construction so as to enable the Engineer to decide whether if these methods are adhered to the Works can be constructed and completed in accordance with the Contract and without detriment to the Permanent Works when completed.

Engineer's consent

(7)   The Engineer shall inform the Contractor in writing within 21 days after receipt of the information submitted in accordance with sub-clauses (1)(b) and (6) of this Clause either

(a)   that the Contractor's proposed methods have the consent of the Engineer or

(b)   in what respects in the opinion of the Engineer they fail to meet the requirements of the Contract or will be detrimental to the Permanent Works.

In the latter event the Contractor shall take such steps or make such changes in the said methods as may be necessary to meet the Engineer's requirements and to obtain his consent. The Contractor shall not change the methods which have received the Engineer's consent without the further consent in writing of the Engineer which shall not be unreasonably withheld.

Delay and extra cost

(8)   If the Contractor unavoidably incurs delay or extra cost because

(a)   the Engineer's consent to the proposed methods of construction is unreasonably delayed or

(b)   the Engineer's requirements pursuant to sub-clause (7) of this Clause or any limitations imposed by any of the design criteria supplied by the Engineer pursuant to sub-clause (5) of this Clause could not reasonably have been foreseen by an experienced contractor at the time of tender

then the Engineer shall take such delay into account in determining any extension of time to which the Contractor is entitled under Clause 44 and the Contractor shall subject to Clause 53 be paid in accordance with Clause 60 the amount of such cost as may be reasonable except to the extent that such delay and extra cost result from the Contractor's default. Profit shall be added thereto in respect of any additional permanent or temporary work.

Responsibility unaffected by acceptance or consent

(9)   Acceptance (or deemed acceptance) by the Engineer of the Contractor's programme in accordance with sub-clauses (2)(3) or (4) of this Clause and the consent of the Engineer to the Contractor's proposed methods of construction in accordance with sub-clause (7) of this Clause shall not relieve the Contractor of any of his duties or responsibilities under the Contract.

Contractor's superintendence   **15**

(1)   The Contractor shall provide all necessary superintendence during the construction and completion of the Works and for as long thereafter as the Engineer may reasonably consider necessary.

Such superintendence shall be given by sufficient persons having adequate knowledge of the operations to be carried out (including the methods and techniques required the hazards likely to be encountered and methods of preventing accidents) for the satisfactory and safe construction of the Works.

Contractor's agent

(2)   The Contractor or a competent and authorized agent or representative approved of in writing by the Engineer (which approval may at any time be withdrawn) is to be constantly on the Works and shall give his whole time to the superintendence of the same.   Such authorized agent or representative shall be in full charge of the Works and shall receive on behalf of the Contractor directions and instructions from the Engineer or (subject to the limitations of Clause 2) the Engineer's Representative.   The Contractor or such authorized agent or representative shall be responsible for the safety of all operations.

Removal of Contractor's employees   **16**

The Contractor shall employ or cause to be employed in and about the construction and completion of the Works and in the superintendence thereof only persons who are careful skilled and experienced in their several trades and callings.

The Engineer shall be at liberty to object to and require the Contractor to remove or cause to be removed from the Works any person employed thereon who in the opinion of the Engineer mis-conducts himself or is incompetent or negligent in the performance of his duties or fails to conform with any particular provisions with regard to safety which may be set out in the Contract or persists in any conduct which is prejudicial to safety or health and such persons shall not be again employed upon the Works without the permission of the Engineer.

Setting out   **17**

(1)   The Contractor shall be responsible for the true and proper setting-out of the Works and for the correctness of the position levels dimensions and alignment of all parts of the Works and for the provision of all necessary instruments appliances and labour in connection therewith.

(2)   If at any time during the progress of the Works any error shall appear or arise in the position levels dimensions or alignment of any part of the Works the Contractor on being required so to do by the Engineer shall at his own cost rectify such error to the satisfaction of the Engineer unless such error is based on incorrect data supplied in writing by the Engineer or the Engineer's Representative in which case the cost of rectifying the same shall be borne by the Employer.

(3)   The checking of any setting-out or of any line or level by the Engineer or the Engineer's Representative shall not in any way relieve the Contractor of his responsibility for the correctness thereof and the Contractor shall carefully protect and preserve all bench-marks sight rails pegs and other things used in setting out the Works.

Boreholes and exploratory excavation 18   If at any time during the construction of the Works the Engineer shall require the Contractor to make boreholes or to carry out exploratory excavation such requirement shall be ordered in writing and shall be deemed to be a variation under Clause 51 unless a Provisional Sum or Prime Cost Item in respect of such anticipated work shall have been included in the Bill of Quantities.

Safety and security 19   (1) The Contractor shall throughout the progress of the Works have full regard for the safety of all persons entitled to be upon the Site and shall keep the Site (so far as the same is under his control) and the Works (so far as the same are not completed or occupied by the Employer) in an orderly state appropriate to the avoidance of danger to such persons and shall among other things in connection with the Works provide and maintain at his own cost all lights guards fencing warning signs and watching when and where necessary or required by the Engineer or the Engineer's Representative or by any competent statutory or other authority for the protection of the Works or for the safety and convenience of the public or others.

Employer's responsibilities   (2) If the Employer carries out work on the Site with his own workpeople he shall in respect of such work

    (a) have full regard for the safety of all persons entitled to be upon the Site and

    (b) keep the Site in an orderly state appropriate to the avoidance of danger to such persons.

If the Employer employs other contractors on the Site he shall require them to have the same regard for safety and avoidance of danger.

Care of the Works 20   (1) (a) The Contractor shall save as in paragraph (b) hereof and subject to sub-clause (2) of this Clause take full responsibility for the care of the Works and materials plant and equipment for incorporation therein from the Works Commencement Date until the date of issue of a Certificate of Substantial Completion for the whole of the Works when the responsibility for the said care shall pass to the Employer.

    (b) If the Engineer issues a Certificate of Substantial Completion for any Section or part of the Permanent Works the Contractor shall cease to be responsible for the care of that Section or part from the date of issue of that Certificate of Substantial Completion when the responsibility for the care of that Section or part shall pass to the Employer.

    (c) The Contractor shall take full responsibility for the care of any work and materials plant and equipment for incorporation therein which he undertakes during the Defects Correction Period until such work has been completed.

Excepted Risks   (2) The Excepted Risks for which the Contractor is not liable are loss or damage to the extent that it is due to

    (a) the use or occupation by the Employer his agents servants or other contractors (not being employed by the Contractor) of any part of the Permanent Works

    (b) any fault defect error or omission in the design of the Works (other than a design provided by the Contractor pursuant to his obligations under the Contract)

    (c) riot war invasion act of foreign enemies or hostilities (whether war be declared or not)

(d)   civil war rebellion revolution insurrection or military or usurped power

(e)   ionizing radiations or contamination by radioactivity from any nuclear fuel or from any nuclear waste from the combustion of nuclear fuel radioactive toxic explosive or other hazardous properties of any explosive nuclear assembly or nuclear component thereof and

(f)   pressure waves caused by aircraft or other aerial devices travelling at sonic or supersonic speeds.

Rectification of loss or damage

(3)   (a)   In the event of any loss or damage to

(i)   the Works or any Section or part thereof or

(ii)   materials plant or equipment for incorporation therein

while the Contractor is responsible for the care thereof (except as provided in sub-clause (2) of this Clause) the Contractor shall at his own cost rectify such loss or damage so that the Permanent Works conform in every respect with the provisions of the Contract and the Engineer's instructions.   The Contractor shall also be liable for any loss or damage to the Works occasioned by him in the course of any operations carried out by him for the purpose of complying with his obligations under Clauses 49 and 50.

(b)   Should any such loss or damage arise from any of the Excepted Risks defined in sub-clause (2) of this Clause the Contractor shall if and to the extent required by the Engineer rectify the loss or damage at the expense of the Employer.

(c)   In the event of loss or damage arising from an Excepted Risk and a risk for which the Contractor is responsible under sub-clause (1)(a) of this Clause then the Engineer shall when determining the expense to be borne by the Employer under the Contract apportion the cost of rectification into that part caused by the Excepted Risk and that part which is the responsibility of the Contractor.

Insurance of Works etc.   21   (1)   The Contractor shall without limiting his or the Employer's obligations and responsibilities under Clause 20 insure in the joint names of the Contractor and the Employer the Works together with materials plant and equipment for incorporation therein to the full replacement cost plus an additional 10% to cover any additional costs that may arise incidental to the rectification of any loss or damage including professional fees cost of demolition and removal of debris.

Extent of cover   (2)   (a)   The insurance required under sub-clause (1) of this Clause shall cover the Employer and the Contractor against all loss or damage from whatsoever cause arising other than the Excepted Risks defined in Clause 20(2) from the Works Commencement Date until the date of issue of the relevant Certificate of Substantial Completion.

(b)   The insurance shall extend to cover any loss or damage arising during the Defects Correction Period from a cause occurring prior to the issue of any Certificate of Substantial Completion and any loss or damage occasioned by the Contractor in the course of any operation carried out by him for the purpose of complying with his obligations under Clauses 49, 50 and 51.

(c)   Nothing in this Clause shall render the Contractor liable to insure against the necessity for the repair or reconstruction of any work constructed with materials or workmanship not in accordance with the requirements of the Contract unless the Bill of Quantities provides a special item for this insurance.

(d)   Any amounts not insured or not recovered from insurers whether as excesses carried under the policy or otherwise shall be borne by the Contractor or the Employer in accordance with their respective responsibilities under Clause 20.

Damage to persons and property   22   (1)   The Contractor shall except if and so far as the Contract provides otherwise and subject to the exceptions set out in sub-clause (2) of this Clause indemnify and keep indemnified the Employer against all losses and claims in respect of

(a)   death of or injury to any person or

(b)   loss of or damage to any property (other than the Works)

which may arise out of or in consequence of the construction of the Works and the remedying of any defects therein and against all claims demands proceedings damages costs charges and expenses whatsoever in respect thereof or in relation thereto.

Exceptions   (2)   The exceptions referred to in sub-clause (1) of this Clause which are the responsibility of the Employer are

(a)   damage to crops being on the Site (save in so far as possession has not been given to the Contractor)

(b)   the use or occupation of land provided by the Employer for the purposes of the Contract (including consequent losses of crops) or interference whether temporary or permanent with any right of way light air or water or other easement or quasi-easement which are the unavoidable result of the construction of the Works in accordance with the Contract

(c)   the right of the Employer to construct the Works or any part thereof on over under in or through any land

(d)   damage which is the unavoidable result of the construction of the Works in accordance with the Contract and

(e)   death of or injury to persons or loss of or damage to property resulting from any act neglect or breach of statutory duty done or committed by the Employer his agents servants or other contractors (not being employed by the Contractor) or for or in respect of any claims demands proceedings damages costs charges and expenses in respect thereof or in relation thereto.

Indemnity by Employer

(3)   The Employer shall subject to sub-clause (4) of this Clause indemnify the Contractor against all claims demands proceedings damages costs charges and expenses in respect of the matters referred to in the exceptions defined in sub-clause (2) of this Clause.

Shared responsibility

(4)   (a)   The Contractor's liability to indemnify the Employer under sub-clause (1) of this Clause shall be reduced in proportion to the extent that the act or neglect of the Employer his agents servants or other contractors (not being employed by the Contractor) may have contributed to the said death injury loss or damage.

(b)   The Employer's liability to indemnify the Contractor under sub-clause (3) of this Clause in respect of matters referred to in sub-clause (2)(e) of this Clause shall be reduced in proportion to the extent that the act or neglect of the Contractor or his sub-contractors servants or agents may have contributed to the said death injury loss or damage.

Third party insurance   23

(1)   The Contractor shall without limiting his or the Employer's obligations and responsibilities under Clause 22 insure in the joint names of the Contractor and the Employer against liabilities for death of or injury to any person (other than any operative or other person in the employment of the Contractor or any of his sub-contractors) or loss of or damage to any property (other than the Works) arising out of the performance of the Contract other than those liabilities arising out of the exceptions defined in Clause 22(2)(a) (b) (c) and (d).

Cross liability clause

(2)   The insurance policy shall include a cross liability clause such that the insurance shall apply to the Contractor and to the Employer as separate insured.

Amount of insurance

(3)   Such insurance shall be for at least the amount stated in the Appendix to the Form of Tender.

**Accident or injury to   24
operatives etc.**

The Employer shall not be liable for or in respect of any damages or compensation payable at law in respect or in consequence of any accident or injury to any operative or other person in the employment of the Contractor or any of his sub-contractors save and except to the extent that such accident or injury results from or is contributed to by any act or default of the Employer his agents or servants and the Contractor shall indemnify and keep indemnified the Employer against all such damages and compensation (save and except as aforesaid) and against all claims demands proceedings costs charges and expenses whatsoever in respect thereof or in relation thereto.

**Evidence and terms   25
of insurance**

(1)   The Contractor shall provide satisfactory evidence to the Employer prior to the Works Commencement Date that the insurances required under the Contract have been effected and shall if so required produce the insurance policies for inspection. The terms of all such insurances shall be subject to the approval of the Employer (which approval shall not unreasonably be withheld). The Contractor shall upon request produce to the Employer receipts for the payment of current insurance premiums.

Excesses

(2)　Any excesses on the policies of insurance effected under Clauses 21 and 23 shall be no greater than those stated in the Appendix to the Form of Tender.

Remedy on Contractor's failure to insure

(3)　If the Contractor shall fail upon request to produce to the Employer satisfactory evidence that there is in force any of the insurances required under the Contract then the Employer may effect and keep in force any such insurance and pay such premium or premiums as may be necessary for that purpose and from time to time deduct the amount so paid from any monies due or which may become due to the Contractor or recover the same as a debt due from the Contractor.

Compliance with policy conditions

(4)　Both the Employer and the Contractor shall comply with all conditions laid down in the insurance policies.　Should the Contractor or the Employer fail to comply with any condition imposed by the insurance policies effected pursuant to the Contract each shall indemnify the other against all losses and claims arising from such failure.

Giving of notices and payment of fees

26　(1)　Except where otherwise provided in the Contract the Contractor shall give all notices and pay all fees required to be given or paid by any Act of Parliament or any Regulation or Bye-law of any local or other statutory authority in relation to the construction and completion of the Works and by the rules and regulations of all public bodies and companies whose property or rights are or may be affected in any way by the Works.

Repayment by Employer

(2)　The Employer shall repay or allow to the Contractor all such sums as the Engineer shall certify to have been properly payable and paid by the Contractor in respect of such fees and also all rates and taxes paid by the Contractor in respect of the Site or any part thereof or anything constructed or erected thereon or on any part thereof or any temporary structures situated elsewhere but used exclusively for the purposes of the Works or any structures used temporarily and exclusively for the purposes of the Works.

Contractor to conform with Statutes etc.

(3)　The Contractor shall ascertain and conform in all respects with the provisions of any general or local Act of Parliament and the Regulations and Bye-laws of any local or other statutory authority which may be applicable to the Works and with such rules and regulations of public bodies and companies as aforesaid and shall keep the Employer indemnified against all penalties and liability of every kind for breach of any such Act Regulation or Bye-law. Provided always that

(a)　the Contractor shall not be required to indemnify the Employer against the consequences of any such breach which is the unavoidable result of complying with the Contract or instructions of the Engineer

(b)　if the Contract or instructions of the Engineer shall at any time be found not to be in conformity with any such Act Regulation or Bye-law the Engineer shall issue such instructions including the ordering of a variation under Clause 51 as may be necessary to ensure conformity with such Act Regulation or Bye-law and

(c)　the Contractor shall not be responsible for obtaining any planning permission which may be necessary in respect of the Permanent Works in their final position or of any Temporary Works designed by the Engineer in their designated position on Site. The Employer hereby warrants that all such permissions have been or will in due time be obtained.

(4)   If the Contractor incurs delay or extra cost arising from matters referred to in sub-clause (3)(b) or failure of the Employer to comply with sub-clause (3)(c) of this Clause the Engineer shall take such delay into account in determining any extension of time to which the Contractor may be entitled under Clause 44 and the Contractor shall subject to Clause 53 be paid in accordance with Clause 60 the amount of such extra cost as may be reasonable except to the extent that such delay or extra cost result from the Contractor's default.

New Roads and Street Works Act 1991— Definitions   27   (1)   (a)   In this Clause "the Act" shall mean the New Roads and Street Works Act 1991 and any statutory modification or re-enactment thereof for the time being in force.

(b)   For the purpose of obtaining any licence under the Act required for the Permanent Works the undertaker shall be the Employer who for the purposes of the Act will be the licensee.

Provided that where the license contains a prohibition against assignment which is notified to the Contractor then the Contractor shall give the Employer all notices required to be given by the undertaker and shall indemnify the Employer from and against all costs and charges which may arise from any failure by him so to do.

(c)   All other expressions common to the Act and to this Clause shall have the same meaning as those assigned to them by the Act.

Licences   (2)   (a)   The Employer shall obtain any street works licence and any other consent licence or permission that may be required for the carrying out of the Permanent Works and shall supply the Contractor with copies thereof including details of any conditions or limitations imposed.

(b)   Any condition or limitation in any licence obtained after the award of the Contract shall be deemed to be an instruction under Clause 13.

Notices   (3)   The Contractor shall be responsible for giving to any relevant authority any required notice (or advance notice where prescribed) of his proposal to commence any work. A copy of each such notice shall be given to the Employer.

Delays attributable to variations   (4)   If any instruction pursuant to sub-clause (2)(b) of this Clause results in delay to the construction and completion of the Works because the Contractor needs to comply with sub-clause (3) of this Clause the Engineer shall in addition to valuing the variation under Clause 52 take such delay into account in determining any extension of time to which the Contractor is entitled under Clause 44 and the Contractor shall subject to Clause 53 be paid in accordance with Clause 60 such additional cost as the Engineer shall consider to have been reasonably attributable to such delay.

Patent rights   28   (1)   The Contractor shall indemnify and keep indemnified the Employer from and against all claims and proceedings for or on account of infringement of any patent right design trademark or name or other protected right in respect of any

(a)   Contractor's Equipment used for or in connection with the Works

(b)   materials plant and equipment for incorporation in the Works

and from and against all claims demands proceedings damages costs charges and expenses whatsoever in respect thereof or in relation thereto except where such infringement results from compliance with the design or Specification provided other than by the Contractor. In the latter event the Employer shall indemnify the Contractor from and against all claims and proceedings for or on account of infringement of any patent right design trademark or name or other protected right aforesaid.

Royalties

(2)   Except where otherwise stated the Contractor shall pay all tonnage and other royalties rent and other payments or compensation (if any) for getting stone sand gravel clay or other materials required for the Works.

Interference with traffic and adjoining properties

29   (1)   All operations necessary for the construction and completion of the Works shall so far as compliance with the requirements of the Contract permits be carried on so as not to interfere unnecessarily or improperly with

(a)   the convenience of the public or

(b)   the access to public or private roads footpaths or properties whether in the possession of the Employer or of any other person and with the use or occupation thereof.

The Contractor shall indemnify and keep indemnified the Employer in respect of all claims demands proceedings damages costs charges and expenses whatsoever arising out of or in relation to any such matters.

Noise disturbance and pollution

(2)   All work shall be carried out without unreasonable noise disturbance or other pollution.

Indemnity by Contractor

(3)   To the extent that noise disturbance or other pollution is not the unavoidable consequence of constructing and completing the Works or performing the Contract the Contractor shall indemnify the Employer from and against any liability for damages on that account and against all claims demands proceedings damages costs charges and expenses whatsoever in regard or in relation to such liability.

Indemnity by Employer

(4)   The Employer shall indemnify the Contractor from and against any liability for damages on account of noise disturbance or other pollution which is the unavoidable consequence of carrying out the Works and from and against all claims demands proceedings damages costs charges and expenses whatsoever in regard or in relation to such liability.

Avoidance of damage to highways etc.

30   (1)   The Contractor shall use every reasonable means to prevent any of the highways or bridges communicating with or on the routes to the Site from being subjected to extraordinary traffic within the meaning of the Highways Act 1980 or in Scotland the Roads (Scotland) Act 1984 or any statutory modification or re-enactment thereof by any traffic of the Contractor or any of his sub-contractors and in particular shall select routes and use vehicles and restrict and distribute loads so that any such extraordinary traffic as will inevitably arise from the moving of Contractor's Equipment and materials or manufactured or fabricated articles from and to the Site shall be limited as far as reasonably possible and so that no unnecessary damage or injury may be occasioned to such highways and bridges.

Transport of Contractor's Equipment

(2)   Save insofar as the Contract otherwise provides the Contractor shall be responsible for and shall pay the cost of strengthening any bridges or altering or improving any highway communicating with the Site to facilitate the movement of Contractor's Equipment or Temporary Works required in the carrying out of the Works and the Contractor shall indemnify and keep indemnified the Employer against all claims for damage to any highway or bridge communicating with the Site caused by such movement including such claims as may be made by any competent authority directly against the Employer pursuant to any Act of Parliament or other Statutory Instrument and shall negotiate and pay all claims arising solely out of such damage.

Transport of materials

(3)   If notwithstanding sub-clause (1) of this Clause any damage occurs to any bridge or highway communicating with the Site arising from the transport of materials or manufactured or fabricated articles being or intended to form part of

the Permanent Works or any Temporary Works designed by the Engineer the Contractor shall notify the Engineer as soon as he becomes aware of such damage or as soon as he receives any claim from the authority entitled to make such claim.

Where under any Act of Parliament or other Statutory Instrument the haulier of such materials or manufactured or fabricated articles is required to indemnify the highway authority against damage the Employer shall not be liable for any costs charges or expenses in respect thereof or in relation thereto.

In other cases the Employer shall negotiate the settlement of and pay all sums due in respect of such claim and shall indemnify the Contractor in respect thereof and in respect of all claims demands proceedings damages costs charges and expenses in relation thereto. Provided always that if and so far as any such claim or part thereof is in the opinion of the Engineer due to any failure on the part of the Contractor to observe and perform his obligations under sub-clause (1) of this Clause then the amount certified by the Engineer to be due to such failure shall be paid by the Contractor to the Employer or deducted from any sum due or which may become due to the Contractor.

Facilities for other contractors 31 (1) The Contractor shall in accordance with the requirements of the Engineer or Engineer's Representative afford all reasonable facilities for any other contractors employed by the Employer and their workmen and for the workmen of the Employer and of any other properly authorised authorities or statutory bodies who may be employed in the carrying out on or near the Site of any work not in the Contract or of any contract which the Employer may enter into in connection with or ancillary to the Works.

Delay and extra cost (2) If compliance with sub-clause (1) of this Clause involves the Contractor in delay or cost beyond that reasonably to have been foreseen by an experienced contractor at the time of tender then the Engineer shall take such delay into account in determining any extension of time to which the Contractor is entitled under Clause 44 and the Contractor shall subject to Clause 53 be paid in accordance with Clause 60 the amount of such cost as may be reasonable. Profit shall be added thereto in respect of any additional permanent or temporary work.

Fossils etc. 32 All fossils coins articles of value or antiquity and structures or other remains or things of geological or archaeological interest discovered on the Site shall as between the Employer and the Contractor be deemed to be the absolute property of the Employer and the Contractor shall take reasonable precautions to prevent his workmen or any other persons from removing or damaging any such article or thing and shall immediately upon discovery thereof and before removal acquaint the Engineer of such discovery and carry out at the expense of the Employer the Engineer's orders as to the disposal of the same.

Clearance of Site on completion 33 On completion of the Works the Contractor shall clear away and remove from the Site all Contractor's Equipment surplus material rubbish and Temporary Works of every kind and leave the whole of the Site and Permanent Works clean and in a workmanlike condition to the satisfaction of the Engineer.

34 (Not used)

Returns of labour and Contractor's Equipment 35 The Contractor shall if required by the Engineer deliver to the Engineer or the Engineer's Representative a return in such form and at such intervals as the Engineer may prescribe showing in detail the numbers of the several classes of labour from time to time employed by the Contractor on the Site and such information respecting Contractor's Equipment as the Engineer may require. The Contractor shall require his sub-contractors to observe the provisions of this Clause.

MATERIALS AND WORKMANSHIP

Quality of materials and workmanship and tests   **36**   (1) All materials and workmanship shall be of the respective kinds described in the Contract and in accordance with the Engineer's instructions and shall be subjected from time to time to such tests as the Engineer may direct at the place of manufacture or fabrication or on the Site or such other place or places as may be specified in the Contract. The Contractor shall provide such assistance instruments machines labour and materials as are normally required for examining measuring and testing any work and the quality weight or quantity of any materials used and shall supply samples of materials before incorporation in the Works for testing as may be selected and required by the Engineer.

Cost of samples   (2) All samples shall be supplied by the Contractor at his own cost if the supply thereof is clearly intended by or provided for in the Contract but if not then at the cost of the Employer.

Cost of tests   (3) The cost of making any test shall be borne by the Contractor if such test is clearly intended by or provided for in the Contract and (in the cases only of a test under load or of a test to ascertain whether the design of any finished or partially finished work is appropriate for the purposes which it was intended to fulfil) is particularized in the Contract in sufficient detail to enable the Contractor to have priced or allowed for the same in his tender.

(4) In all other cases the cost of making any test shall be borne by the Employer unless the need for such test results from the Contractor's default or from failure on the part of the Contractor to observe and perform his obligations under the Contract.

Access to site   **37**   The Engineer and any person authorized by him shall at all times have access to the Works and to the Site and to all workshops and places where work is being prepared or whence materials manufactured articles and machinery are being obtained for the Works and the Contractor shall afford every facility for and every assistance in obtaining such access or the right to such access.

Examination of work before covering up   **38**   (1) No work shall be covered up or put out of view without the consent of the Engineer and the Contractor shall afford full opportunity for the Engineer to examine and measure any work which is about to be covered up or put out of view and to examine foundations before permanent work is placed thereon. The Contractor shall give due notice to the Engineer whenever any such work or foundations is or are ready or about to be ready for examination and the Engineer shall without unreasonable delay unless he considers it unnecessary and advises the Contractor accordingly attend for the purpose of examining and measuring such work or of examining such foundations.

Uncovering and making openings

(2) The Contractor shall uncover any part or parts of the Works or make openings in or through the same as the Engineer may from time to time direct and shall reinstate and make good such part or parts to the satisfaction of the Engineer. If any such part or parts have been covered up or put out of view after compliance with the requirements of sub-clause (1) of this Clause and are found to have been carried out in accordance with the Contract the cost of uncovering making openings in or through reinstating and making good the same shall be borne by the Employer but in any other case all such cost shall be borne by the Contractor.

Removal of unsatisfactory work and materials

39 (1) The Engineer shall during the progress of the Works have power to instruct in writing the

    (a) removal from the Site within such time or times specified in the instruction of any materials which in the opinion of the Engineer are not in accordance with the Contract

    (b) substitution with materials in accordance with the Contract and

    (c) removal and proper replacement (notwithstanding any previous test thereof or interim payment therefor) of any work which in respect of

        (i) material or workmanship or

        (ii) design by the Contractor or for which he is responsible

is not in the opinion of the Engineer in accordance with the Contract.

Default of Contractor in compliance

(2) In case of default on the part of the Contractor in carrying out such instruction the Employer shall be entitled to employ and pay other persons to carry out the same and all costs consequent thereon or incidental thereto as determined by the Engineer shall be recoverable from the Contractor by the Employer and may be deducted by the Employer from any monies due or to become due to him and the Engineer shall notify the Contractor accordingly with a copy to the Employer.

Failure to disapprove

(3) Failure of the Engineer or any person acting under him pursuant to Clause 2 to disapprove any work or materials shall not prejudice the power of the Engineer or any such person subsequently to take action under this Clause.

Suspension of work

40 (1) The Contractor shall on the written order of the Engineer suspend the progress of the Works or any part thereof for such time or times and in such manner as the Engineer may consider necessary and shall during such suspension properly protect and secure the work so far as is necessary in the opinion of the Engineer. Except to the extent that such suspension is

    (a) otherwise provided for in the Contract or

    (b) necessary by reason of weather conditions or by some default on the part of the Contractor or

    (c) necessary for the proper construction and completion or for the safety of the Works or any part thereof in as much as such necessity does not arise from any act or default of the Engineer or the Employer or from any of the Excepted Risks defined in Clause 20(2) then if compliance with the Engineer's instructions under this clause involves the Contractor in delay or extra cost the Engineer shall take such delay into account in determining any extension of time to which the Contractor is entitled under Clause 44 and the Contractor shall subject to Clause 53 be paid in accordance with Clause 60 the amount of such extra cost as may be reasonable. Profit shall be added thereto in respect of any additional permanent or temporary work.

Suspension lasting more than three months

(2)   If the progress of the Works or any part thereof is suspended on the written order of the Engineer and if permission to resume work is not given by the Engineer within a period of 3 months from the date of suspension then the Contractor may unless such suspension is otherwise provided for in the Contract or continues to be necessary by reason of some default on the part of the Contractor serve a written notice on the Engineer requiring permission within 28 days from the receipt of such notice to proceed with the Works or that part thereof in regard to which progress is suspended. If within the said 28 days the Engineer does not grant such permission the Contractor by a further written notice so served may (but is not bound to) elect to treat the suspension where it affects part only of the Works as an omission of such part under Clause 51 or where it affects the whole Works as an abandonment of the Contract by the Employer.

COMMENCEMENT TIME AND DELAYS

Works Commencement Date   **41**   (1)   The Works Commencement Date shall be

(a)   the date specified in the Appendix to the Form of Tender or if no date is specified

(b)   a date between 14 and 28 days of the award of the Contract to be notified to the Contractor by the Engineer in writing or

(c)   such other date as may be agreed between the parties.

Start of Works

(2)   The Contractor shall start the Works on or as soon as is reasonably practicable after the Works Commencement Date. Thereafter the Contractor shall proceed with the Works with due expedition and without delay in accordance with the Contract.

Possession of Site and access   **42**   (1)   The Contract may prescribe

(a)   the extent of portions of the Site of which the Contractor is to be given possession from time to time

(b)   the order in which such portions of the Site shall be made available to the Contractor

(c)   the availability and the nature of the access which is to be provided by the Employer

(d)   the order in which the Works shall be constructed.

(2) (a)   Subject to sub-clause (1) of this Clause the Employer shall give to the Contractor on the Works Commencement Date possession of the whole of the Site together with such access thereto as may be necessary to enable the Contractor to commence and proceed with the construction of the Works.

(b)   Thereafter the Employer shall during the course of the Works give to the Contractor such further access in accordance with the Contract as is necessary to enable the Contractor to proceed with the construction of the Works with due despatch.

Failure to give possession

(3)   If the Contractor suffers delay and/or incurs extra cost from failure on the part of the Employer to give possession or access in accordance with the terms of this Clause the Engineer shall take such delay into account in determining any extension of time to which the Contractor is entitled under Clause 44 and the Contractor shall subject to Clause 53 be paid in accordance with Clause 60 the amount of any extra cost to which he may be entitled. Profit shall be added thereto in respect of any additional permanent or temporary work.

Access and facilities provided by the Contractor

(4)   The Contractor shall bear all costs and charges for any access required by him additional to those provided by the Employer. The Contractor shall also provide at his own cost any additional facilities outside the Site required by him for the purposes of the Works.

Time for completion   **43**

The whole of the Works and any Section required to be completed within a particular time as stated in the Appendix to the Form of Tender shall be substantially completed within the time so stated (or such extended time as may be allowed under Clause 44 or revised time agreed under Clause 46(3)) calculated from the Works Commencement Date.

Extension of time for completion   **44**

(1)   Should the Contractor consider that

(a)   any variation ordered under Clause 51(1) or

(b)   increased quantities referred to in Clause 51(4) or

(c)   any cause of delay referred to in these Conditions or

(d)   exceptional adverse weather conditions or

(e)   any delay impediment prevention or default by the Employer or

(f)   other special circumstances of any kind whatsoever which may occur

be such as to entitle him to an extension of time for the substantial completion of the Works or any Section thereof he shall within 28 days after the cause of any delay has arisen or as soon thereafter as is reasonable deliver to the Engineer full and detailed particulars in justification of the period of extension claimed in order that the claim may be investigated at the time.

Assessment of delay

(2) (a) The Engineer shall upon receipt of such particulars consider all the circumstances known to him at that time and make an assessment of the delay (if any) that has been suffered by the Contractor as a result of the alleged cause and shall so notify the Contractor in writing.

(b) The Engineer may in the absence of any claim make an assessment of the delay that he considers has been suffered by the Contractor as a result of any of the circumstances listed in sub-clause (1) of this Clause and shall so notify the Contractor in writing.

Interim grant of extension of time

(3) Should the Engineer consider that the delay suffered fairly entitles the Contractor to an extension of the time for the substantial completion of the Works or any Section thereof such interim extension shall be granted forthwith and be notified to the Contractor in writing with a copy to the Employer. In the event that the Contractor has made a claim for an extension of time but the Engineer does not consider the Contractor entitled to an extension of time he shall so inform the Contractor without delay.

Assessment at due date for completion

(4) The Engineer shall not later than 14 days after the due date or extended date for completion of the Works or any Section thereof (and whether or not the Contractor shall have made any claim for an extension of time) consider all the circumstances known to him at that time and take action similar to that provided for in sub-clause (3) of this Clause. Should the Engineer consider that the Contractor is not entitled to an extension of time he shall so notify the Employer and the Contractor.

Final determination of extension

(5) The Engineer shall within 28 days of the issue of the Certificate of Substantial Completion for the Works or for any Section thereof review all the circumstances of the kind referred to in sub-clause (1) of this Clause and shall finally determine and certify to the Contractor with a copy to the Employer the overall extension of time (if any) to which he considers the Contractor entitled in respect of the Works or the relevant Section. No such final review of the circumstances shall result in a decrease in any extension of time already granted by the Engineer pursuant to sub-clauses (3) or (4) of this Clause.

Night and Sunday work   45

Subject to any provision to the contrary contained in the Contract none of the Works shall be carried out during the night or on Sundays without the permission in writing of the Engineer save when the work is unavoidable or absolutely necessary for the saving of life or property or for the safety of the Works in which case the Contractor shall immediately advise the Engineer or the Engineer's Representative. Provided always that this Clause shall not be applicable in the case of any work which it is customary to carry out outside normal working hours or by rotary or double shifts.

Rate of progress   46

(1) If for any reason which does not entitle the Contractor to an extension of time the rate of progress of the Works or any Section is at any time in the opinion of the Engineer too slow to ensure substantial completion by the time or extended time for completion prescribed by Clause 43 and 44 as appropriate or the revised time for completion agreed under sub-clause (3) of this Clause the Engineer shall notify the Contractor in writing and the Contractor shall thereupon take such steps as are necessary and to which the Engineer may consent to expedite the progress so as substantially to complete the Works or such Section by that prescribed time or extended time. The Contractor shall not be entitled to any additional payment for taking such steps.

Permission to work at night or on Sundays

(2) If as a result of any notice given by the Engineer under sub-clause (1) of this Clause the Contractor seeks the Engineer's permission to do any work on Site at night or on Sundays such permission shall not be unreasonably refused.

Provision for accelerated completion

(3) If the Contractor is requested by the Employer or the Engineer to complete the Works or any Section within a revised time being less than the time or extended time for completion prescribed by Clauses 43 and 44 as appropriate and the Contractor agrees so to do then any special terms and conditions of payment shall be agreed between the Contractor and the Employer before any such action is taken.

LIQUIDATED DAMAGES FOR DELAY

Liquidated damages for delay in substantial completion of the whole of the Works

47 (1) (a) Where the whole of the Works is not divided into Sections the Appendix to the Form of Tender shall include a sum which represents the Employer's genuine pre-estimate (expressed per week or per day as the case may be) of the damages likely to be suffered by him if the whole of the Works is not substantially completed within the time prescribed by Clause 43 or by any extension thereof granted under Clause 44 or by any revision thereof agreed under Clause 46(3) as the case may be.

(b) If the Contractor fails to achieve substantial completion of the whole of the Works within the time so prescribed he shall pay to the Employer the said sum for every week or day (as the case may be) which shall elapse between the date on which the prescribed time expired and the date the whole of the Works is substantially completed.

Provided that if any part of the Works is certified as substantially complete pursuant to Clause 48 before the completion of the whole of the Works the said sum shall be reduced by the proportion which the value of the part so completed bears to the value of the whole of the Works.

Liquidated damages for delay in substantial completion where the whole of the Works is divided into Sections

(2) (a) Where the Works is divided into Sections (together comprising the whole of the Works) which are required to be completed within particular times as stated in the Appendix to the Form of Tender sub-clause (1) of this Clause shall not apply and the said Appendix shall include a sum in respect of each Section which represents the Employer's genuine pre-estimate (expressed per week or per day as the case may be) of the damages likely to be suffered by him if that Section is not substantially completed within the time prescribed by Clause 43 or by any extension thereof granted under Clause 44 or by any revision thereof agreed under Clause 46(3) as the case may be.

(b) If the Contractor fails to achieve substantial completion of any Section within the time so prescribed he shall pay to the Employer the appropriate stated sum for every week or day (as the case may be) which shall elapse between the date on which the prescribed time expired and the date of substantial completion of that Section.

Provided that if any part of that Section is certified as substantially complete pursuant to Clause 48 before the completion of the whole thereof the appropriate stated sum shall be reduced by the proportion which the value of the part so completed bears to the value of the whole of that Section.

(c)   Liquidated damages in respect of two or more Sections may where circumstances so dictate run concurrently.

Damages not a penalty

(3)   All sums payable by the Contractor to the Employer pursuant to this Clause shall be paid as liquidated damages for delay and not as a penalty.

Limitation of liquidated damages

(4)   (a)   The total amount of liquidated damages in respect of the whole of the Works or any Section thereof shall be limited to the appropriate sum stated in the Appendix to the Form of Tender. If no such limit is stated therein then liquidated damages without limit shall apply.

(b)   Should there be omitted from the Appendix to the Form of Tender any sum required to be inserted therein either by sub-clause (1)(a) or by sub-clause (2)(a) of this Clause as the case may be or if any such sum is stated to be "nil" then to that extent damages shall not be payable.

Recovery and reimbursement of liquidated damages

(5)   The Employer may

(a)   deduct and retain the amount of any liquidated damages becoming due under the provision of this Clause from any sums due or which become due to the Contractor or

(b)   require the Contractor to pay such amount to the Employer forthwith.

If upon a subsequent or final review of the circumstances causing delay the Engineer grants a relevant extension or further extension of time the Employer shall no longer be entitled to liquidated damages in respect of the period of such extension.

Any sum in respect of such period which may already have been recovered under this Clause shall be reimbursed forthwith to the Contractor together with interest compounded monthly at the rate provided for in Clause 60(7) from the date on which such sums were recovered from the Contractor.

Intervention of variations etc.

(6)   If after liquidated damages have become payable in respect of any part of the Works the Engineer orders a variation under Clause 51 or adverse physical conditions or artificial obstructions within the meaning of Clause 12 are encountered or any other situation outside the Contractor's control arises any of which in the Engineer's opinion results in further delay to that part of the Works

(a)   the Engineer shall so notify the Contractor and the Employer in writing and

(b)   the Employer's further entitlement to liquidated damages in respect of that part of the Works shall be suspended until the Engineer notifies the Contractor and the Employer in writing that the further delay has come to an end.

Such suspension shall not invalidate any entitlement to liquidated damages which accrued before the period of further delay started to run and subject to any subsequent or final review of the circumstances causing delay any monies already deducted or paid as liquidated damages under the provision of this Clause may be retained by the Employer.

CERTIFICATE OF SUBSTANTIAL COMPLETION

Notification of substantial completion   **48**   (1)   When the Contractor considers that

    (a)   the whole of the Works or

    (b)   any Section in respect of which a separate time for completion is provided in the Appendix to the Form of Tender

has been substantially completed and has satisfactorily passed any final test that may be prescribed by the Contract he may give notice in writing to that effect to the Engineer or to the Engineer's Representative. Such notice shall be accompanied by an undertaking to finish any outstanding work in accordance with the provisions of Clause 49(1).

Certification of substantial completion   (2)   The Engineer shall within 21 days of the date of delivery of such notice either

    (a)   issue to the Contractor (with a copy to the Employer) a Certificate of Substantial Completion stating the date on which in his opinion the Works were or the Section was substantially completed in accordance with the Contract or

    (b)   give instructions in writing to the Contractor specifying all the work which in the Engineer's opinion requires to be done by the Contractor before the issue of such certificate.

If the Engineer gives such instructions the Contractor shall be entitled to receive a Certificate of Substantial Completion within 21 days of completion to the satisfaction of the Engineer of the work specified in the said instructions.

Premature use by Employer   (3)   If any substantial part of the Works has been occupied or used by the Employer other than as provided in the Contract the Contractor may request in writing and the Engineer shall issue a Certificate of Substantial Completion in respect thereof. Such certificate shall take effect from the date of delivery of the Contractor's request and upon the issue of such certificate the Contractor shall be deemed to have undertaken to complete any outstanding work in that part of the Works during the Defects Correction Period.

Substantial completion of other parts of the Works   (4)   If the Engineer considers that any part of the Works has been substantially completed and has passed any final test that may be prescribed by the Contract he may issue a Certificate of Substantial Completion in respect of that part of the Works before completion of the whole of the Works and upon the issue of such certificate the Contractor shall be deemed to have undertaken to complete any outstanding work in that part of the Works during the Defects Correction Period.

Reinstatement of ground   (5)   A Certificate of Substantial Completion given in respect of any Section or part of the Works before completion of the whole shall not be deemed to certify completion of any ground or surfaces requiring reinstatement unless such certificate shall expressly so state.

OUTSTANDING WORK AND DEFECTS

Work outstanding   **49**   (1)   The undertaking to be given under Clause 48(1) may after agreement between the Engineer and the Contractor specify a time or times within which the outstanding work shall be completed. If no such times are specified any outstanding work shall be completed as soon as practicable during the Defects Correction Period.

Carrying out of work of repair etc.   (2)   The Contractor shall deliver up to the Employer the Works and each Section and part thereof at or as soon as practicable after the end of the relevant Defects Correction Period in the condition required by the Contract (fair wear and tear excepted) to the satisfaction of the Engineer. To this end the Contractor shall as soon as practicable carry out all work of repair amendment reconstruction rectification and making good of defects of whatever nature as may be required of him in writing by the Engineer during the relevant Defects Correction Period or within 14 days after its expiry as a result of an inspection made by or on behalf of the Engineer prior to its expiry.

Cost of work of repair etc.   (3)   All work required under sub-clause (2) of this Clause shall be carried out by the Contractor at his own expense if in the Engineer's opinion it is necessary due to the use of materials or workmanship not in accordance with the Contract or to neglect or failure by the Contractor to comply with any of his obligations under the Contract. In any other event the value of such work shall be ascertained and paid for as if it were additional work.

Remedy on Contractor's failure to carry out work required   (4)   If the Contractor fails to do any such work as aforesaid the Employer shall be entitled to carry out that work by his own workpeople or by other contractors and if it is work which the Contractor should have carried out at his own expense the Employer shall be entitled to recover the cost thereof from the Contractor and may deduct the same from any monies that are or may become due to the Contractor.

Contractor to search   **50**   The Contractor shall if required by the Engineer in writing carry out such searches tests or trials as may be necessary to determine the cause of any defect imperfection or fault under the directions of the Engineer. Unless the defect imperfection or fault is one for which the Contractor is liable under the Contract the cost of the work carried out by the Contractor as aforesaid shall be borne by the Employer. If the defect imperfection or fault is one for which the Contractor is liable the cost of the work carried out as aforesaid shall be borne by the Contractor and he shall in such case repair rectify and make good such defect imperfection or fault at his own expense in accordance with Clause 49.

ALTERATIONS, ADDITIONS AND OMISSIONS

Ordered variations   **51**   (1)   The Engineer

(a)   shall order any variation to any part of the Works that is in his opinion necessary for the completion of the Works and

(b)   may order any variation that for any other reason shall in his opinion be desirable for the completion and/or improved functioning of the Works.

Such variations may include additions omissions substitutions alterations changes in quality form character kind position dimension level or line and changes in any specified sequence method or timing of construction required by the Contract and may be ordered during the Defects Correction Period.

Ordered variations to be in writing

(2) All variations shall be ordered in writing but the provisions of Clause 2(6) in respect of oral instructions shall apply.

Variation not to affect Contract

(3) No variation ordered in accordance with sub-clauses (1) and (2) of this Clause shall in any way vitiate or invalidate the Contract but the value (if any) of all such variations shall be taken into account in ascertaining the amount of the Contract Price except to the extent that such variation is necessitated by the Contractor's default.

Changes in quantities

(4) No order in writing shall be required for increase or decrease in the quantity of any work where such increase or decrease is not the result of an order given under this Clause but is the result of the quantities exceeding or being less than those stated in the Bill of Quantities.

Valuation of ordered variations   **52**

(1) If requested by the Engineer the Contractor shall submit his quotation for any proposed variation and his estimate of any consequential delay. Wherever possible the value and delay consequences (if any) of each variation shall be agreed before the order is issued or before work starts.

(2) Where a request is not made or agreement is not reached under sub-clause (1) the valuation of variations ordered by the Engineer in accordance with Clause 51 shall be ascertained as follows.

    (a) As soon as possible after receipt of the variation the Contractor shall submit to the Engineer

        (i) his quotation for any extra or substituted works necessitated by the variation having due regard to any rates or prices included in the Contract and

        (ii) his estimate of any delay occasioned thereby and

        (iii) his estimate of the cost of any such delay.

    (b) Within 14 days of receiving the said submissions the Engineer shall

        (i) accept those submissions or

        (ii) negotiate with the Contractor thereon.

    (c) Upon reaching agreement with the Contractor the Contract Price shall be amended accordingly.

(3) Failing agreement between the Engineer and the Contractor under either sub-clause (1) or (2) the value of variations ordered by the Engineer in accordance with Clause 51 shall be ascertained by the Engineer in accordance with the following principles and be notified to the Contractor.

(a) Where work is of similar character and carried out under similar conditions to work priced in the Bill of Quantities it shall be valued at such rates and prices contained therein as may be applicable.

(b) Where work is not of a similar character or is not carried out under similar conditions or is ordered during the Defects Correction Period the rates and prices in the Bill of Quantities shall be used as the basis for valuation so far as may be reasonable failing which a fair valuation shall be made.

Engineer to fix rates

(4) If in the opinion of the Engineer or the Contractor any rate or price contained in the Contract for any item of work (not being the subject of any variation) is by reason of any variation rendered unreasonable or inapplicable either the Engineer shall give to the Contractor or the Contractor shall give to the Engineer notice before the varied work is commenced or as soon thereafter as is reasonable in all the circumstances that such rate or price should be increased or decreased and the Engineer shall fix such rate or price as in the circumstances he shall think reasonable and proper and shall so notify the Contractor.

Daywork

(5) The Engineer may if in his opinion it is necessary or desirable order in writing that any additional or substituted work shall be carried out on a daywork basis in accordance with the provisions of Clause 56(4).

Additional payments 53

(1) If the Contractor intends to claim a higher rate or price than one notified to him by the Engineer pursuant to sub-clauses (3) and (4) of Clause 52 or Clause 56(2) the Contractor shall within 28 days after such notification give notice in writing of his intention to the Engineer.

(2) If the Contractor intends to claim any additional payment pursuant to any Clause of these Conditions other than sub-clauses (3) and (4) of Clause 52 or Clause 56(2) he shall give notice in writing of his intention to the Engineer as soon as may be reasonable and in any event within 28 days after the happening of the events giving rise to the claim.

Upon the happening of such events the Contractor shall keep such contemporary records as may reasonably be necessary to support any claim he may subsequently wish to make.

(3) Without necessarily admitting the Employer's liability the Engineer may upon receipt of a notice under this Clause instruct the Contractor to keep such contemporary records or further contemporary records as the case may be as are reasonable and may be material to the claim of which notice has been given and the Contractor shall keep such records.

The Contractor shall permit the Engineer to inspect all records kept pursuant to Clause 53 and shall supply him with copies thereof as and when the Engineer shall so instruct.

(4)   After the giving of a notice to the Engineer under this Clause the Contractor shall as soon as is reasonable in all the circumstances send to the Engineer a first interim account giving full and detailed particulars of the amount claimed to that date and of the grounds upon which the claim is based.

Thereafter at such intervals as the Engineer may reasonably require the Contractor shall send to the Engineer further up to date accounts giving the accumulated total of the claim and any further grounds upon which it is based.

(5)   If the Contractor fails to comply with any of the provisions of this Clause in respect of any claim which he shall seek to make then the Contractor shall be entitled to payment in respect thereof only to the extent that the Engineer has not been prevented from or substantially prejudiced by such failure in investigating the said claim.

(6)   The Contractor shall be entitled to have included in any interim payment certified by the Engineer pursuant to Clause 60 such amount in respect of any claim as the Engineer may consider due to the Contractor provided that the Contractor shall have supplied sufficient particulars to enable the Engineer to determine the amount due.

If such particulars are insufficient to substantiate the whole of the claim the Contractor shall be entitled to payment in respect of such part of the claim as the particulars may substantiate to the satisfaction of the Engineer.

PROPERTY IN MATERIALS AND CONTRACTOR'S EQUIPMENT

Non-removal of Materials and Contractor's Equipment

54   (1)   No Contractor's Equipment Temporary Works materials for Temporary Works or other goods or materials owned by the Contractor and brought on to the Site for the purposes of the Contract shall be removed without the written consent of the Engineer which consent shall not unreasonably be withheld.

Liability for loss or damage to Contractor's Equipment

(2)   The Employer shall not at any time be liable save as mentioned in Clauses 20(2) and 63 for the loss of or damage to any Contractor's Equipment Temporary Works goods or materials.

Disposal of Contractor's Equipment

(3)   If the Contractor fails to remove any of the said Contractor's Equipment Temporary Works goods or materials as required by Clause 33 within such reasonable time after completion of the Works as the Engineer may allow then the Employer may sell or otherwise dispose of such items. From the proceeds of the sale of any such items the Employer shall be entitled to retain any costs or expenses incurred in connection with their sale and disposal before paying the balance (if any) to the Contractor.

Vesting of goods and materials not on Site

(4)   With a view to securing payment under Clause 60(1)(c) the Contractor may (and shall if the Engineer so directs) transfer to the Employer the property in goods and materials listed in the Appendix to the Form of Tender or as subsequently agreed between the Contractor and the Employer before the same are delivered to the Site provided that the goods and materials

(a)   have been manufactured or prepared and are substantially ready for incorporation in the Works and

(b)   are the property of the Contractor or the contract for the supply of the same expressly provides that the property therein shall pass unconditionally to the Contractor upon the Contractor taking the action referred to in sub-clause (5) of this Clause and

(c)   have been marked and set aside in accordance with sub-clause (5) of this Clause.

Action by Contractor

(5)   The intention of the Contractor to transfer the property in any goods or materials to the Employer in accordance with this Clause shall be evidenced by the Contractor taking or causing the supplier of those goods or materials to take the following actions.

(a)   Provide to the Engineer documentary evidence that the property of the said goods or materials has vested in the Contractor.

(b)   Suitably mark or otherwise plainly identify the goods and materials so as to show that their destination is the Site that they are the property of the Employer and (where they are not stored at the premises of the Contractor) to whose order they are held.

(c)   Set aside and store the said goods and materials so marked and identified to the satisfaction of the Engineer.

(d)   Send to the Engineer a schedule listing and giving the value of every item of the goods and materials so set aside and stored and inviting him to inspect them.

Vesting in the Employer

(6)   Upon the Engineer approving in writing the transfer in ownership of any goods and materials for the purposes of this Clause they shall vest in and become the absolute property of the Employer and thereafter shall be in the possession of the Contractor for the sole purpose of delivering them to the Employer and incorporating them in the Works and shall not be within the ownership control or disposition of the Contractor. Provided always that

(a)   approval by the Engineer for the purposes of this Clause or any payment certified by him in respect of goods and materials pursuant to Clause 60 shall be without prejudice to the exercise of any power of the Engineer contained in this Contract to reject any goods or materials which are not in accordance with the provisions of the Contract and upon any such rejection the property in the rejected goods or materials shall immediately re-vest in the Contractor and

(b)   the Contractor shall be responsible for any loss or damage to such goods or materials and for the cost of storing handling and transporting the same and shall effect such additional insurance as may be necessary to cover the risk of such loss or damage from any cause.

Lien on goods and materials

(7)   Neither the Contractor nor a sub-contractor nor any person shall have a lien on any goods or materials which have vested in the Employer under sub-clause (6) of this Clause for any sum due to the Contractor sub-contractor or other person and the Contractor shall take all steps reasonably necessary to ensure that the title of the Employer and the exclusion of any such lien are brought to the notice of sub-contractors and other persons dealing with such goods or materials.

Delivery to the Employer of vested goods or materials

(8)   Upon cessation of the employment of the Contractor under this Contract before the completion of the Works whether as a result of the operation of Clause 63 64 or 65 or otherwise the Contractor shall deliver to the Employer any goods or materials the property in which has vested in the Employer by virtue of sub-clause (6) of this Clause and if he fails to do so the Employer may enter any premises of the Contractor or of any sub-contractor and remove such goods and materials and recover the cost of doing so from the Contractor.

Incorporation in sub-contracts

(9)   The Contractor shall incorporate provisions equivalent to those provided in this Clause in every sub-contract in which provision is to be made for the payment in respect of goods or materials before the same have been delivered to the Site.

MEASUREMENT

Quantities   55

(1)   The quantities set out in the Bill of Quantities are the estimated quantities of the work but they are not to be taken as the actual and correct quantities of the Works to be carried out by the Contractor in fulfilment of his obligations under the Contract.

Correction of errors

(2)   No error in description in the Bill of Quantities or omission therefrom shall vitiate the Contract nor release the Contractor from the carrying out of the whole or any part of the Works according to the Drawings and Specification or from any of his obligations or liabilities under the Contract. Any such error or omission shall be corrected by the Engineer and the value of the work actually carried out shall be ascertained in accordance with Clause 52(2) or (3). Provided that there shall be no rectification of any errors omissions or wrong estimates in the descriptions rates and prices inserted by the Contractor in the Bill of Quantities.

Measurement and valuation   56

(1)   The Engineer shall except as otherwise stated ascertain and determine by admeasurement the value in accordance with the Contract of the work done in accordance with the Contract.

Increase or decrease of rate

(2)   Should the actual quantities carried out in respect of any item be greater or less than those stated in the Bill of Quantities and if in the opinion of the Engineer such increase or decrease of itself shall so warrant the Engineer shall after consultation with the Contractor determine an appropriate increase or decrease of any rates or prices rendered unreasonable or inapplicable in consequence thereof and shall notify the Contractor accordingly.

Attending for measurement

(3)   The Engineer shall when he requires any part or parts of the work to be measured give reasonable notice to the Contractor who shall attend or send a qualified agent to assist the Engineer or the Engineer's Representative in making such measurement and shall furnish all particulars required by either of them. Should the Contractor not attend or neglect or omit to send such agent then the measurement made by the Engineer or approved by him shall be taken to be the correct measurement of the work.

Daywork

(4)   Where any work is carried out on a daywork basis the Contractor shall be paid for such work under the conditions and at the rates and prices set out in the daywork schedule included in the Contract or failing the inclusion of a daywork schedule he shall be paid at the rates and prices and under the conditions contained in the "Schedules of Dayworks carried out incidental to Contract Work" issued by The Civil Engineering Contractors Association (formerly issued by The Federation of Civil Engineering Contractors) current at the date of the carrying out of the daywork.

The Contractor shall furnish to the Engineer such records receipts and other documentation as may be necessary to prove amounts paid and/or costs incurred. Such returns shall be in the form and delivered at the times the Engineer shall direct and shall be agreed within a reasonable time.

Before ordering materials the Contractor shall if so required submit to the Engineer quotations for the same for his approval.

Method of measurement   **57**

Unless otherwise provided in the Contract or unless general or detailed description of the work in the Bill of Quantities or any other statement clearly shows to the contrary the Bill of Quantities shall be deemed to have been prepared and measurements shall be made according to the procedure set out in the "Civil Engineering Standard Method of Measurement Third Edition 1991" approved by the Institution of Civil Engineers and the Federation of Civil Engineering Contractors in association with the Association of Consulting Engineers or such later or amended edition thereof as may be stated in the Appendix to the Form of Tender to have been adopted in its preparation.

PROVISIONAL AND PRIME COST SUMS AND NOMINATED SUB-CONTRACTS

Use of Provisional Sums   **58**

(1)   In respect of every Provisional Sum the Engineer may order either or both of the following.

(a)   Work to be carried out or goods materials or services to be supplied by the Contractor the value thereof being determined in accordance with Clause 52 and included in the Contract Price.

(b)   Work to be carried out or goods materials or services to be supplied by a Nominated Sub-contractor in accordance with Clause 59.

Use of Prime Cost Items

(2)   In respect of every Prime Cost Item the Engineer may order either or both of the following.

(a)   Subject to Clause 59 that the Contractor employ a sub-contractor nominated by the Engineer for the carrying out of any work or the supply of any goods materials or services included therein.

(b)   With the consent of the Contractor that the Contractor himself carry out any such work or supply any such goods materials or services in which event the Contractor shall be paid in accordance with the terms of a quotation submitted by him and accepted by the Engineer or in the absence thereof the value shall be determined in accordance with Clause 52 and included in the Contract Price.

Design requirements to be expressly stated

(3)   If in connection with any Provisional Sum or Prime Cost Item the services to be provided include any matter of design or specification of any part of the Permanent Works or of any equipment or plant to be incorporated therein such requirement shall be expressly stated in the Contract and shall be included in any Nominated Sub-contract. The obligation of the Contractor in respect thereof shall be only that which has been expressly stated in accordance with this sub-clause.

Nominated Sub-contractors — objection to nomination   **59**   (1)   The Contractor shall not be under any obligation to enter into a sub-contract with any Nominated Sub-contractor against whom the Contractor may raise reasonable objection or who declines to enter into a sub-contract with the Contractor containing provisions

(a)   that in respect of the work goods materials or services the subject of the sub-contract the Nominated Sub-contractor will undertake towards the Contractor such obligations and liabilities as will enable the Contractor to discharge his own obligations and liabilities towards the Employer under the terms of the Contract

(b)   that the Nominated Sub-contractor will indemnify and keep indemnified the Contractor against all claims demands and proceedings damages costs charges and expenses whatsoever arising out of or in connection with any failure by the Nominated Sub-contractor to perform such obligations or fulfil such liabilities

(c)   that the Nominated Sub-contractor will indemnify and keep indemnified the Contractor from and against any negligence by the Nominated Sub-contractor his agents workmen and servants and against any misuse by him or them of any Contractor's Equipment or Temporary Works provided by the Contractor for the purposes of the Contract and for all claims as aforesaid

(d)   that the Nominated Sub-contractor will provide the Contractor with security for the proper performance of the sub-contract and

(e)   equivalent to those contained in Clause 63.

Engineer's action upon objection to nomination or upon determination of Nominated Sub-contract

(2)   If pursuant to sub-clause (1) of this Clause the Contractor declines to enter into a sub-contract with a sub-contractor nominated by the Engineer or if during the course of the Nominated Sub-contract the Contractor shall validly terminate the employment of the Nominated Sub-contractor as a result of his default the Engineer shall

(a)   nominate an alternative sub-contractor in which case sub-clause (1) of this Clause shall apply or

(b)   by order under Clause 51 vary the Works or the work goods materials or services in question or

(c)   by order under Clause 51 omit any or any part of such works goods materials or services so that they may be provided by workmen contractors or suppliers employed by the Employer either

(i)   concurrently with the Works (in which case Clause 31 shall apply) or

(ii)   at some other date

and in either case there shall nevertheless be included in the Contract Price such sum (if any) in respect of the Contractor's charges and profit being a percentage of the estimated value of such omission as would have been payable had there been no such omission and the value thereof had been that estimated in the Bill of Quantities or inserted in the Appendix to the Form of Tender as the case may be or

(d)   instruct the Contractor to secure a sub-contractor of his own choice and to submit a quotation for the work goods materials or services in question to be so performed or provided for the Engineer's consideration and action or

(e)   invite the Contractor himself to carry out or supply the work goods materials or services in question under Clause 58(1)(a) or Clause 58(2)(b) or on a daywork basis as the case may be.

Contractor responsible for Nominated Sub-contractors

(3)   Except as otherwise provided in Clause 58 (3) the Contractor shall be as responsible for the work carried out or goods materials or services supplied by a Nominated Sub-contractor employed by him as if he had himself carried out such work or supplied such goods materials or services.

Nominated Sub-contractor's default

(4)   (a)   If any event arises which in the opinion of the Contractor justifies the exercise of his right under any forfeiture clause to terminate the sub-contract or to treat the sub-contract as repudiated by the Nominated Sub-contractor he shall at once notify the Engineer in writing giving his reasons.

Termination of Sub-contract

(b)   With the consent in writing of the Engineer the Contractor may give notice to the Nominated Sub-contractor expelling him from the Sub-contract works pursuant to any forfeiture clause or rescinding the Sub-contract as the case may be. If however the Engineer's consent is withheld the Contractor shall be entitled to appropriate instructions under Clause 13.

Engineer's action upon termination

(c)   In the event that the Nominated Sub-contractor is expelled from the Sub-contract works the Engineer shall at once take such action as is required under sub-clause (2) of this Clause.

Recovery of additional expense

(d)   Having with the Engineer's consent terminated the Nominated Sub-contract the Contractor shall take all necessary steps and proceedings as are available to him to recover all additional expenses that are incurred from the Sub-contractor or under the security provided pursuant to sub-clause (1)(d) of this Clause. Such expenses shall include any additional expenses incurred by the Employer as a result of the termination.

Reimbursement of Contractor's loss

(e)   If and to the extent that the Contractor fails to recover all his reasonable expenses of completing the Sub-contract works and all his proper additional expenses arising from the termination the Employer will reimburse the Contractor his unrecovered expenses.

Consequent delay

(f)   The Engineer shall take any delay to the completion of the Works consequent upon the Nominated Sub-contractor's default into account in determining any extension of time to which the Contractor is entitled under Clause 44.

Provisions for payment

(5)   For all work carried out or goods materials or services supplied by Nominated Sub-contractors there shall be included in the Contract Price

(a)   the actual price paid or due to be paid by the Contractor in accordance with the terms of the sub-contract (unless and to the extent that any such payment is the result of a default of the Contractor) net of all trade and other discounts, rebates and allowances other than any discount obtainable by the Contractor for prompt payment

(b)   the sum (if any) provided in the Bill of Quantities for labours in connection therewith and

(c)   in respect of all other charges and profit a sum being a percentage of the actual price paid or due to be paid calculated (where provision has been made in the Bill of Quantities for a rate to be set against the relevant item of prime cost) at the rate inserted by the Contractor against that item or (where no such provision has been made) at the rate inserted by the Contractor in the Appendix to the Form of Tender as the percentage for adjustment of sums set against Prime Cost Items.

Production of vouchers etc.

(6)   The Contractor shall when required by the Engineer produce all quotations invoices vouchers sub-contract documents accounts and receipts in connection with expenditure in respect of work carried out by all Nominated Sub-contractors.

Payment to Nominated Sub-contractors

(7)   Before issuing any certificate under Clause 60 the Engineer shall be entitled to demand from the Contractor reasonable proof that all sums (less retentions provided for in the Sub-contract) included in previous certificates in respect of the work carried out or goods or materials or services supplied by Nominated Sub-contractors have been paid to the Nominated Sub-contractors or discharged by the Contractor in default whereof unless the Contractor shall

(a)   give details to the Engineer in writing of any reasonable cause he may have for withholding or refusing to make such payment and

(b)   produce to the Engineer reasonable proof that he has so informed such Nominated Sub-contractor in writing

the Employer shall be entitled to pay to such Nominated Sub-contractor direct upon the certification of the Engineer all payments (less retentions provided for in the Sub-contract) which the Contractor has failed to make to such Nominated Sub-contractor and to deduct by way of set-off the amount so paid by the Employer from any sums due or which become due from the Employer to the Contractor. Provided always that where the Engineer has certified and the Employer has made direct payment to the Nominated Sub-contractor the Engineer shall in issuing any further certificate in favour of the Contractor deduct from the amount thereof the amount so paid but shall not withhold or delay the issue of the certificate itself when due to be issued under the terms of the Contract.

CERTIFICATES AND PAYMENT

Monthly statements   **60**   (1) Unless otherwise agreed the Contractor shall submit to the Engineer at monthly intervals commencing one month after the Works Commencement Date a statement (in such form if any as may be prescribed in the Specification) showing

> (a) the estimated contract value of the Permanent Works carried out up to the end of that month
>
> (b) a list of any goods or materials delivered to the Site for but not yet incorporated in the Permanent Works and their value
>
> (c) a list of any of those goods or materials identified in the Appendix to the Form of Tender which have not yet been delivered to the Site but of which the property has vested in the Employer pursuant to Clause 54 and their value and
>
> (d) the estimated amounts to which the Contractor considers himself entitled in connection with all other matters for which provision is made under the Contract including any Temporary Works or Contractor's Equipment for which separate amounts are included in the Bill of Quantities

unless in the opinion of the Contractor such values and amounts together will not justify the issue of an interim certificate.

Amounts payable in respect of Nominated Sub-contracts are to be listed separately.

Monthly payments   (2) Within 25 days of the date of delivery of the Contractor's monthly statement to the Engineer or the Engineer's Representative in accordance with sub-clause (1) of this Clause the Engineer shall certify and within 28 days of the same date the Employer shall pay to the Contractor (after deducting any previous payments on account)

> (a) the amount which in the opinion of the Engineer on the basis of the monthly statement is due to the Contractor on account of sub-clauses (1)(a) and (1)(d) of this Clause less a retention as provided in sub-clause (5) of this Clause and
>
> (b) such amounts (if any) as the Engineer may consider proper (but in no case exceeding the percentage of the value stated in the Appendix to the Form of Tender) in respect of sub-clauses (1)(b) and (1)(c) of this Clause.

The payments become due on certification with the final date for payment being 28 days after the date of delivery of the Contractor's monthly statement.

The amounts certified in respect of Nominated Sub-contracts shall be shown separately in the certificate.

Minimum amount of certificate

(3) Until the whole of the Works has been certified as substantially complete in accordance with Clause 48 the Engineer shall not be bound to issue an interim certificate for a sum less than that stated in the Appendix to the Form of Tender but thereafter he shall be bound to do so and the certification and payment of amounts due to the Contractor shall be in accordance with the time limits contained in this Clause.

Final account

(4) Not later than 3 months after the date of the Defects Correction Certificate the Contractor shall submit to the Engineer a statement of final account and supporting documentation showing in detail the value in accordance with the Contract of the Works carried out together with all further sums which the Contractor considers to be due to him under the Contract up to the date of the Defects Correction Certificate.

Within 3 months after receipt of this final account and of all information reasonably required for its verification the Engineer shall issue a certificate stating the amount which in his opinion is finally due under the Contract from the Employer to the Contractor or from the Contractor to the Employer as the case may be up to the date of the Defects Correction Certificate and after giving credit to the Employer for all amounts previously paid by the Employer and for all sums to which the Employer is entitled under the Contract.

Such amount shall subject to Clause 47 be paid to or by the Contractor as the case may require. The payment becomes due on certification. The final date for payment is 28 days later.

Retention

(5) The retention to be made pursuant to sub-clause (2)(a) of this Clause shall be the difference between

(a) an amount calculated at the rate indicated in and up to the limit set out in the Appendix to the Form of Tender upon the amount due to the Contractor on account of sub-clauses (1)(a) and (1)(d) of this Clause and

(b) any payment which shall have become due under sub-clause (6) of this Clause.

Payment of retention

(6) (a) Upon the issue of a Certificate of Substantial Completion in respect of any Section or part of the Works there shall become due to the Contractor one half of such proportion of the amount calculated to date under sub-clause (5)(a) of this Clause as the value of the Section or part bears to the value of the whole of the Works completed to date as certified under sub-clause (2)(a) of this Clause.

The total of the payments which shall become due under this sub-clause shall in no event exceed one half of the limit of retention set out in the Appendix to the Form of Tender.

(b) Upon issue of the Certificate of Substantial Completion in respect of the whole of the Works there shall become due to the Contractor one half of the amount calculated in accordance with sub-clause (5)(a) of this Clause less any payments which shall have become due under sub-clause (6)(a) of this Clause. Within 10 days of the date of issue of the said Certificate the Engineer shall certify the amount due.

Payment becomes due on certification of the amount due with the final date for payment being 14 days after the issue of the Certificate of Substantial Completion.

(c)   At the end of the Defects Correction Period or if more than one the last of such periods there shall become due to the Contractor the remainder of the retention money. Within 10 days of the date of the end of the said period the Engineer shall certify the amount due.

Payment becomes due on certification of the amount due with the final date for payment being 14 days after the end of the said period notwithstanding that at that time there may be outstanding claims by the Contractor against the Employer.

Provided that if at that time there remains to be carried out by the Contractor any outstanding work referred to under Clause 48 or any work ordered pursuant to Clauses 49 or 50 the Engineer may withhold certification until the completion of such work of so much of the said remainder as shall in the opinion of the Engineer represent the cost of the work remaining to be carried out.

Interest on overdue payments

(7)   In the event of

(a)   failure by the Engineer to certify or the Employer to make payment in accordance with sub-clauses (2) (4) or (6) of this Clause or

(b)   any decision of an adjudicator or any finding of an arbitrator to such effect

the Employer shall pay to the Contractor interest compounded monthly for each day on which any payment is overdue or which should have been certified and paid at a rate equivalent to 2% per annum above the base lending rate of the bank specified in the Appendix to the Form of Tender.

If in an arbitration pursuant to Clause 66 the arbitrator holds that any sum or additional sum should have been certified by a particular date in accordance with the aforementioned sub-clauses but was not so certified this shall be regarded for the purposes of this sub-clause as a failure to certify such sum or additional sum. Such sum or additional sum shall be regarded as overdue for payment 28 days after the date by which the arbitrator holds that the Engineer should have certified the sum or if no such date is identified by the arbitrator shall be regarded as overdue for payment from the date of the Certificate of Substantial Completion for the whole of the Works.

Correction and withholding of certificates

(8)   The Engineer shall have power to omit from any certificate the value of any work done goods or materials supplied or services rendered with which he may for the time being be dissatisfied and for that purpose or for any other reason which to him may seem proper may by any certificate delete correct or modify any sum previously certified by him. Provided that

(a)   the Engineer shall not in any interim certificate delete or reduce any sum previously certified in respect of work done goods or materials supplied or services rendered by a Nominated Sub-contractor if the Contractor shall have already paid or be bound to pay that sum to the Nominated Sub-contractor and

(b)   if the Engineer in the final certificate shall delete or reduce any sum previously certified in respect of work done goods or materials supplied or services rendered by a Nominated Sub-contractor which sum shall have been already paid by the Contractor to the Nominated Sub-contractor the Employer shall reimburse to the Contractor the amount of any sum overpaid by the Contractor to the Sub-contractor in accordance with the certificates issued under sub-clause (2) of this Clause which the Contractor shall be unable to recover from the Nominated Sub-contractor together with interest thereon at the rate stated in sub-clause (7) of this Clause from 28 days after the date of the final certificate issued under sub-clause (4) of this Clause until the date of such reimbursement.

Certificates and payment notices

(9)   Every certificate issued by the Engineer pursuant to this Clause shall be sent to the Employer and on the Employer's behalf to the Contractor.   By this certificate the Employer shall give notice to the Contractor specifying the amount (if any) of the payment proposed to be made and the basis on which it was calculated.

Notice of intention to withhold payment

(10) Where a payment under Clause 60(2) (4) or (6) is to differ from that certified or the Employer is to withhold payment after the final date for payment of a sum due under the Contract the Employer shall notify the Contractor in writing not less than one day before the final date for payment specifying the amount proposed to be withheld and the ground for withholding payment or if there is more than one ground each ground and the amount attributable to it.

Defects Correction Certificate   61

(1)   At the end of the Defects Correction Period or if more than one the last of such periods and when all outstanding work referred to under Clause 48 and all work of repair amendment reconstruction rectification and making good of defects imperfections shrinkages and other faults referred to under Clauses 49 and 50 have been completed the Engineer shall issue to the Employer (with a copy to the Contractor) a Defects Correction Certificate stating the date on which the Contractor shall have completed his obligations to construct and complete the Works to the Engineer's satisfaction.

Unfulfilled obligations

(2)   The issue of the Defects Correction Certificate shall not be taken as relieving either the Contractor or the Employer from any liability the one towards the other arising out of or in any way connected with the performance of their respective obligations under the Contract.

REMEDIES AND POWERS

Urgent repairs   62

If in the opinion of the Engineer any remedial or other work or repair is urgently necessary by reason of any accident or failure or other event occurring to in or in connection with the Works or any part thereof either during the carrying out of the Works or during the Defects Correction Period the Engineer shall so inform the Contractor with confirmation in writing.

Thereafter if the Contractor is unable or unwilling to carry out such work or repair at once the Employer may himself carry out the said work or repair using his own or other workpeople.

If the work or repair so carried out by the Employer is work which in the opinion of the Engineer the Contractor was liable to carry out at his own expense under the Contract all costs and charges properly incurred by the Employer in so doing shall on demand be paid by the Contractor to the Employer or may be deducted by the Employer from any monies due or which may become due to the Contractor.

Frustration **63** (1) If any circumstance outside the control of both parties arises during the currency of the Contract which renders it impossible or illegal for either party to fulfil his contractual obligations the Works shall be deemed to be abandoned upon the service by one party upon the other of written notice to that effect.

War clause (2) If during the currency of the Contract there is an outbreak of war (whether war is declared or not) in which Great Britain is engaged on a scale involving general mobilization of the armed forces of the Crown

    (a) the Contractor shall for a period of 28 days reckoned from midnight on the date that the order for general mobilization is given continue so far as is physically possible to carry out the Works in accordance with the Contract and

    (b) if substantial completion of the whole of the Works is not achieved before the said period of 28 days has expired the Works shall thereupon be deemed to be abandoned unless the parties otherwise agree.

Removal of Contractor's Equipment (3) Upon abandonment of the Works pursuant to sub-clauses (1) or (2)(b) of this Clause the Contractor shall with all reasonable dispatch remove from the Site all Contractor's Equipment.

In the event of any failure so to do the Employer shall have like powers to those contained in clause 54(3) to dispose of any Contractor's Equipment.

Payment on abandonment (4) Upon abandonment of the Works pursuant to sub-clauses (1) or (2)(b) of this Clause the Employer shall pay the Contractor (in so far as such amounts or items have not already been covered by payments on account made to the Contractor) the Contract value of all work carried out prior to the date of abandonment and in addition

    (a) the amounts payable in respect of any preliminary items so far as the work or service comprised therein has been carried out or performed and a proper proportion of any such items which have been partially carried out or performed

    (b) the cost of materials or goods reasonably ordered for the Works which have been delivered to the Contractor or of which the Contractor is legally liable to accept delivery (such materials or goods becoming the property of the Employer upon such payment being made to the Contractor)

    (c) a sum being the amount of any expenditure reasonably incurred by the Contractor in the expectation of completing the whole of the Works insofar as such expenditure has not been recovered by any other payments referred to in this sub-clause and

    (d) the reasonable cost of removal under sub-clause (3) of this Clause.

To this end and without prejudice to the provisions of sub-clause (5) of this Clause the provisions of Clause 60(4) shall apply to this sub-clause as if the date of abandonment was the date of issue of the Defects Correction Certificate.

Works substantially completed (5) If upon abandonment of the Works any Section or part of the Works has been substantially completed in accordance with Clause 48 or is completed so far as to be usable then in connection therewith

(a)   the Contractor may at his discretion and in lieu of his obligations under Clauses 49 and 50 allow against the sum due to him pursuant to sub-clause (4) of this Clause the cost (calculated as at the date of abandonment) of repair rectification and making good for which he would have been liable under the said Clauses had they continued to be applicable and

(b)   the Employer shall not be entitled to withhold payment under Clause 60(6)(c) of the second half of the retention money or any part thereof except such sum as the Contractor may allow under the provisions of the last preceding paragraph.

Contract to continue in force
(6)   Save as aforesaid the Contract shall continue to have full force and effect.

Default of the Employer
64   (1)   In the event that the Employer

(a)   assigns or attempts to assign the Contract or any part thereof or any benefit or interest thereunder without the prior written consent of the Contractor or

(b)   (i)   becomes bankrupt or presents his petition in bankruptcy or

(ii)   has a receiving order or administration order made against him or

(iii)   makes an arrangement with or an assignment in favour of his creditors or

(iv)   agrees to perform the Contract under a committee of inspection of his creditors or

(v)   (being a corporation) has a receiver or administrator appointed or goes into liquidation (other than a voluntary liquidation for the purposes of amalgamation or reconstruction) or

(c)   has an execution levied on his goods which is not stayed or discharged within 28 days

then the Contractor may after giving 7 days notice in writing to the Employer specifying the event relied on terminate his employment under the Contract without thereby avoiding the Contract or releasing the Employer from any of his obligations or liabilities under the Contract.

Provided that the Contractor may extend the period of notice to give the Employer an opportunity to remedy the situation.

Removal of Contractor's Equipment
(2)   Upon expiry of the 7 days notice referred to in sub-clause (1) of this Clause and notwithstanding the provisions of Clause 54 the Contractor shall with all reasonable despatch remove from the site all Contractor's Equipment.

Payment upon termination

(3)   Upon termination of the Contractor's employment pursuant to sub-clause (1) of this Clause the Employer shall be under the same obligations with regard to payment as if the Works had been abandoned under the provisions of Clause 63.

Provided that in addition to payments specified under Clause 63(4) the Employer shall pay to the Contractor the amount of any loss or damage to the Contractor arising from or as a consequence of such termination.

Default of Contractor   65   (1)   In the event that the Contractor

(a)   assigns or attempts to assign the Contract or any part thereof or any benefit or interest thereunder without the prior written consent of the Employer or

(b)   is in breach of Clause 4(1) or

(c)   (i)   becomes bankrupt or presents his petition in bankruptcy or

(ii)   has a receiving order or administration order made against him or

(iii)   makes an arrangement with or an assignment in favour of his creditors or

(iv)   agrees to carry out the Contract under a committee of inspection of his creditors or

(v)   (being a corporation) has a receiver or administrator appointed or goes into liquidation (other than a voluntary liquidation for the purposes of amalgamation or reconstruction) or

(d)   has an execution levied on his goods which is not stayed or discharged within 28 days

or if the Engineer certifies in writing to the Employer with a copy to the Contractor that in his opinion the Contractor

(e)   has abandoned the Contract without due cause or

(f)   without reasonable excuse has failed to commence the Works in accordance with Clause 41 or

(g)   has suspended the progress of the Works without due cause for 14 days after receiving from the Engineer written notice to proceed or

(h)   has failed to remove goods or materials from the Site or to pull down and replace work for 14 days after receiving from the Engineer written notice that the said goods materials or work has been condemned and rejected by the Engineer or

(j)   despite previous warnings by the Engineer in writing is failing to proceed with the Works with due diligence or is otherwise persistently or fundamentally in breach of his obligations under the Contract then the Employer may after giving 7 days notice in writing to the Contractor specifying the event relied on enter upon the Works and any other parts of the Site provided by the Employer and expel the Contractor therefrom without thereby avoiding the Contract or releasing the Contractor from any of his obligations or liabilities under the Contract.

Where a notice of termination is given pursuant to a certificate issued by the Engineer under this sub-clause it shall be given as soon as is reasonably possible after receipt of the certificate.

Provided that the Employer may extend the period of notice to give the Contractor an opportunity to remedy the situation.

Completing the Works

(2)   Where the Employer has entered upon the Works and any other parts of the Site as set out in sub-clause (1) of this Clause he may

    (a)   complete the Works himself or

    (b)   employ any other contractor to complete the Works

and in either case may use for such completion any of the Contractor's Equipment Temporary Works goods and materials on any part of the Site.

The Employer may at any time sell any of the said Contractor's Equipment Temporary Works and unused goods and materials and apply the proceeds of sale in or towards the satisfaction of any sums due or which may become due to him from the Contractor under the Contract.

Assignment to Employer

(3)   Where the Employer has entered upon the Works and any other parts of the Site as hereinbefore provided the Contractor shall if so instructed by the Engineer in writing within 7 days of such entry assign to the Employer the benefit of any agreement which the Contractor may have entered into for the supply of any goods or materials and/or for the carrying out of any work for the purposes of the Contract.

Valuation at date of termination

(4)   As soon as may be practicable after any such entry and expulsion by the Employer the Engineer shall fix and determine as at the time of such entry and expulsion

    (a)   the amount (if any) which has been reasonably earned by or would reasonably accrue to the Contractor in respect of work actually done by him under the Contract and

    (b)   the value of any unused or partially used goods and materials which are under the control of the Employer

and shall certify accordingly.

The said determination may be carried out *ex parte* or by or after reference to the parties or after such investigation or enquiry as the Engineer may think fit to make or institute.

Payment after termination

(5) (a)   If the Employer enters and expels the Contractor under this Clause he shall not be liable to pay the Contractor any money under the Contract (whether in respect of amounts certified by the Engineer or otherwise) unless or until the Engineer certifies that an amount is due to the Contractor under sub-clause (b).

(b)   The Engineer shall certify the difference between

(i)   such sum as would have been due to the Contractor if he had completed the Works together with any proceeds of sale under sub-clause 2 of this Clause and

(ii)   the costs of completing the Works (whether or not the Works are completed under a separate contract) damages for delay (if any) and all other expenses properly incurred by the Employer.

(c)   Such difference as is certified by the Engineer in sub-clause (b) shall be a debt due to the Employer or Contractor as the case may be.

(d)   If the Engineer is satisfied at any time prior to the completion of the Works that such sum as calculated under sub-clause (b)(ii) exceeds such sum as calculated under sub-clause (b)(i) he may issue an interim certificate to that effect notwithstanding that the Works have not been completed and such interim certificate shall be considered a debt due from the Contractor to the Employer.

(e)   Every certificate issued by the Engineer pursuant to this Clause shall be sent to the Employer and at the same time copied to the Contractor with such detailed explanation as may be necessary.

AVOIDANCE AND SETTLEMENT OF DISPUTES

Avoidance of disputes   66   (1)   In order to overcome where possible the causes of disputes and in those cases where disputes are likely still to arise to facilitate their clear definition and early resolution (whether by agreement or otherwise) the following procedure shall apply for the avoidance and settlement of disputes.

Matters of dissatisfaction

(2)   If at any time

(a)   the Contractor is dissatisfied with any act or instruction of the Engineer's Representative or any other person responsible to the Engineer or

(b)   the Employer or the Contractor is dissatisfied with any decision opinion instruction direction certificate or valuation of the Engineer or with any other matter arising under or in connection with the Contract or the carrying out of the Works

the matter of dissatisfaction shall be referred to the Engineer who shall notify his written decision to the Employer and the Contractor within one month of the reference to him.

Disputes

(3)   The Employer and the Contractor agree that no matter shall constitute nor be said to give rise to a dispute unless and until in respect of that matter

(a)   the time for the giving of a decision by the Engineer on a matter of dissatisfaction under Clause 66(2) has expired or the decision given is unacceptable or has not been implemented and in consequence the Employer or the Contractor has served on the other and on the Engineer a notice in writing (hereinafter called the Notice of Dispute)

(b)   an adjudicator has given a decision on a dispute under Clause 66(6) and the Employer or the Contractor is not giving effect to the decision, and in consequence the other has served on him and the Engineer a Notice of Dispute

and the dispute shall be that stated in the Notice of Dispute. For the purposes of all matters arising under or in connection with the Contract or the carrying out of the Works the word "dispute" shall be construed accordingly and shall include any difference.

(4)   (a)   Notwithstanding the existence of a dispute following the service of a Notice under Clause 66(3) and unless the Contract has already been determined or abandoned the Employer and the Contractor shall continue to perform their obligations.

(b)   The Employer and the Contractor shall give effect forthwith to every decision of

(i)   the Engineer on a matter of dissatisfaction given under Clause 66(2) and

(ii)   the adjudicator on a dispute given under Clause 66(6)

unless and until that decision is revised by agreement of the Employer and Contractor or pursuant to Clause 66.

Conciliation

Thomas 1993

(5)   (a)   The Employer or the Contractor may at any time before service of a Notice to Refer to arbitration under Clause 66(9) by notice in writing seek the agreement of the other for the dispute to be considered under "The Institution of Civil Engineers' Conciliation Procedure 1999" or any amendment or modification thereof being in force at the date of such notice.

(b)   If the other party agrees to this procedure any recommendation of the conciliator shall be deemed to have been accepted as finally determining the dispute by agreement so that the matter is no longer in dispute unless a Notice of Adjudication under Clause 66(6) or a Notice to Refer to arbitration under Clause 66(9) has been served in respect of that dispute not later than one month after receipt of the recommendation by the dissenting party.

Adjudication

(6)   (a)   The Employer and the Contractor each has the right to refer a dispute as to a matter under the Contract for adjudication and either party may give notice in writing (hereinafter called the Notice of Adjudication) to the other at any time of his intention so to do. The adjudication shall be conducted under "The Institution of Civil Engineers' Adjudication Procedure 1997" or any amendment or modification thereof being in force at the time of the said Notice.

(b)   Unless the adjudicator has already been appointed he is to be appointed by a timetable with the object of securing his appointment and referral of the dispute to him within 7 days of such notice.

(c)   The adjudicator shall reach a decision within 28 days of referral or such longer period as is agreed by the parties after the dispute has been referred.

(d)   The adjudicator may extend the period of 28 days by up to 14 days with the consent of the party by whom the dispute was referred.

(e)   The adjudicator shall act impartially.

(f)   The adjudicator may take the initiative in ascertaining the facts and the law.

(7)   The decision of the adjudicator shall be binding until the dispute is finally determined by legal proceedings or by arbitration (if the contract provides for arbitration or the parties otherwise agree to arbitration) or by agreement.

(8)   The adjudicator is not liable for anything done or omitted in the discharge or purported discharge of his functions as adjudicator unless the act or omission is in bad faith and any employee or agent of the adjudicator is similarly not liable.

Arbitration

(9)   (a)   All disputes arising under or in connection with the Contract or the carrying out of the Works other than failure to give effect to a decision of an adjudicator shall be finally determined by reference to arbitration. The party seeking arbitration shall serve on the other party a notice in writing (called the Notice to Refer) to refer the dispute to arbitration.

(b)   Where an adjudicator has given a decision under Clause 66(6) in respect of the particular dispute the Notice to Refer must be served within three months of the giving of the decision otherwise it shall be final as well as binding.

Appointment of arbitrator

(10)   (a)   The arbitrator shall be a person appointed by agreement of the parties.

President or Vice-President to act

(b)   If the parties fail to appoint an arbitrator within one month of either party serving on the other party a notice in writing (hereinafter called the Notice to Concur) to concur in the appointment of an arbitrator the dispute shall be referred to a person to be appointed on the application of either party by the President for the time being of the Institution of Civil Engineers.

(c)   If an arbitrator declines the appointment or after appointment is removed by order of a competent court or is incapable of acting or dies and the parties do not within one month of the vacancy arising fill the vacancy then either party may apply to the President for the time being of the Institution of Civil Engineers to appoint another arbitrator to fill the vacancy.

(d)   In any case where the President for the time being of the Institution of Civil Engineers is not able to exercise the functions conferred on him by this Clause the said functions shall be exercised on his behalf by a Vice-President for the time being of the said Institution.

Arbitration — procedure and powers

(11)   (a)   Any reference to arbitration under this Clause shall be deemed to be a submission to arbitration within the meaning of the Arbitration Act 1996 or any statutory re-enactment or amendment thereof for the time being in force. The reference shall be conducted in accordance with the procedure set out in the Appendix to the Form of Tender or any amendment or modification thereof being in force at the time of the appointment of the arbitrator. Such arbitrator shall have full power to open up review and revise any decision opinion instruction direction certificate or valuation of the Engineer or an adjudicator.

(b)   Neither party shall be limited in the arbitration to the evidence or arguments put to the Engineer or to any adjudicator pursuant to Clause 66(2) or 66(6) respectively.

(c)   The award of the arbitrator shall be binding on all parties.

(d)   Unless the parties otherwise agree in writing any reference to arbitration may proceed notwithstanding that the Works are not then complete or alleged to be complete.

Witnesses   (12) (a)   No decision opinion instruction direction certificate or valuation given by the Engineer shall disqualify him from being called as a witness and giving evidence before a conciliator adjudicator or arbitrator on any matter whatsoever relevant to the dispute.

(b)   All matters and information placed before a conciliator pursuant to a reference under sub-clause (5) of this Clause shall be deemed to be submitted to him without prejudice and the conciliator shall not be called as witness by the parties or anyone claiming through them in connection with any adjudication arbitration or other legal proceedings arising out of or connected with any matter so referred to him.

APPLICATION TO SCOTLAND AND NORTHERN IRELAND

Application to Scotland   67   (1)   If the Works are situated in Scotland the Contract shall in all respects be construed and operate as a Scottish contract and shall be interpreted in accordance with Scots Law and the provisions of sub-clause (2) of this Clause shall apply.

(2)   In the application of these Conditions and in particular Clause 66 thereof

(a)   the word "arbiter" shall be substituted for the word "arbitrator"

(b)   for any reference to the "Arbitration Act 1996" there shall be substituted reference to the law of Scotland and/or Section 66 and Schedule 7 of the "Law Reform (Miscellaneous Provisions) (Scotland) Act 1990" as may be appropriate

(c)   for any reference to "The Institution of Civil Engineers' Arbitration Procedure (1997)" or "The Construction Industry Model Arbitration Rules" there shall be substituted a reference to "The Institution of Civil Engineers Arbitration Procedure (Scotland) (1983)" or any amendment or modification thereof being in force at the time of the appointment of the arbiter

(d)   notwithstanding any of the other provisions of these Conditions nothing therein shall be construed as excluding or otherwise affecting the right of a party to arbitration to call in terms of Section 3 of the Administration of Justice (Scotland) Act 1972 for the arbiter to state a case and

(e)   where the Employer or the Contractor wishes to register the decision of an adjudicator in the Books of Council and Session for preservation and execution the other party shall on being requested to do so forthwith consent to such registration by subscribing the said decision before a witness.

Application to Northern Ireland   (3)   If the Works are situated in Northern Ireland the Contract shall in all respects be construed and operate as a Northern Irish contract and shall be interpreted in accordance with the law of Northern Ireland.

Application elsewhere   (4)   If the Works are situated in a country or jurisdiction other than England and

Wales Scotland or Northern Ireland the Contract and the provisions for disputes settlement shall in all respects be construed and operate and be interpreted in accordance with the law of that country or jurisdiction.

NOTICES

Service of notices on Contractor   **68**   (1)   Any notice to be given to the Contractor under the terms of the Contract shall be served in writing at the Contractor's principal place of business (or in the event of the Contractor being a Company to or at its registered office).

Service of notices on Employer   (2)   Any notice to be given to the Employer under the terms of the Contract shall be served in writing at the Employer's last known address (or in the event of the Employer being a Company to or at its registered office).

(3)   Any notice to be given by or to the Engineer under the terms of the Contract shall be delivered as the Engineer may direct.

TAX MATTERS

Labour-tax and landfill tax fluctuations   **69**   (1)   The rates and prices contained in the Bill of Quantities shall be deemed to take account only of the levels and incidence in force at the date for return of tenders of

(a)   the taxes levies contributions premiums or refunds (including national insurance contributions but excluding income tax and any levy payable under the Industrial Training Act 1982 or any statutory re-enactment or amendment thereof for the time being in force) which are by law payable by or to the Contractor and his sub-contractors in respect of their workpeople engaged on the Contract and

(b)   any landfill tax payable by the Contractor or his sub-contractors pursuant to the Finance Act 1996 (Sections 39-71 and Schedule 5) and the Landfill Tax Regulations 1996 or any statutory re-enactment or amendment thereof for the time being in force

and shall not take account of any level or incidence of the aforesaid matters foreseeable or known to take effect at some later date.

(2)   If after the date for return of tenders there shall occur any change in the level and/or incidence of any such taxes levies contributions premiums or refunds the Contractor shall so inform the Engineer and the net increase or decrease shall be taken into account in arriving at the Contract Price. The Contractor shall supply the information necessary to support any consequent adjustment to the Contract Price. All certificates for payment issued after submission of such information shall take due account of the additions or deductions to which such information relates.

Value Added Tax   **70**   (1)   The Contractor shall be deemed not to have allowed in his tender for the tax payable by him as a taxable person to the Commissioners of Customs and Excise being tax chargeable on any taxable supplies to the Employer which are to be made under the Contract.

Engineer's certificates net of Value Added Tax   (2)   All certificates issued by the Engineer under Clause 60 shall be net of Value Added Tax.

In addition to the payments due under such certificates the Employer shall separately identify and pay to the Contractor any Value Added Tax properly chargeable by the Commissioners of Customs and Excise on the supply to the Employer of any goods and/or services by the Contractor under the Contract.

Disputes

(3)   If any dispute difference or question arises between either the Employer or the Contractor and the Commissioners of Customs and Excise in relation to any tax chargeable or alleged to be chargeable in connection with the Contract or the Works each shall render to the other such support and assistance as may be necessary to resolve the dispute difference or question.

Clause 66 not applicable

(4)   Clause 66 shall not apply to any dispute difference or question arising under this Clause.

THE CONSTRUCTION (DESIGN AND MANAGEMENT) REGULATIONS 1994

CDM Regulations 1994   71

(1)   In this clause

(a)   "the Regulations" means the Construction (Design and Management) Regulations 1994 or any statutory re-enactment or amendment thereof for the time being in force

(b)   "Planning Supervisor" and "Principal Contractor" mean the persons so described in regulation 2(1) of the Regulations

(c)   "Health and Safety Plan" means the plan prepared by virtue of regulation 15 of the Regulations.

(2)   Where and to the extent that the Regulations apply to the Works and

(a)   the Engineer is appointed Planning Supervisor and/or

(b)   the Contractor is appointed Principal Contractor

then in taking any action as such they shall state in writing that the action is being taken under the Regulations.

(3)   (a)   Any action under the Regulations taken by either the Planning Supervisor or the Principal Contractor and in particular any alteration or amendment to the Health and Safety Plan shall be deemed to be an Engineer's instruction pursuant to Clause 13. Provided that the Contractor shall in no event be entitled to any additional payment and/or extension of time in respect of any such action to the extent that it results from any action lack of action or default on the part of the Contractor.

(b)   If any such action of either the Planning Supervisor or the Principal Contractor could not in the Contractor's opinion reasonably have been foreseen by an experienced contractor the Contractor shall as early as practicable give written notice thereof to the Engineer.

SPECIAL CONDITIONS

Special conditions   72

The following special conditions form part of the Conditions of Contract.

(Note. Any special conditions including Contract Price Fluctuation which it is desired to incorporate in the Conditions of Contract should be numbered consecutively with the foregoing conditions of contract).

SHORT DESCRIPTION OF WORKS

All Permanent and Temporary Works in connection with* ………..

....

....

Form of Tender

(NOTE: The Appendix forms part of the Form of Tender)

To ………..

....

....

GENTLEMEN,

Having examined the Drawings, Conditions of Contract, Specification and Bill of Quantities for the construction of the above-mentioned Works (and the matters set out in the Appendix hereto) we offer to construct and complete the whole of the said Works in conformity with the said Drawings, Conditions of Contract, Specification and Bill of Quantities for such sum as may be ascertained in accordance with the said Conditions of Contract.

We undertake to complete and deliver the whole of the Permanent Works comprised in the Contract within the time stated in the Appendix hereto.

If our Tender is accepted we will, if required, provide security for the due performance of the Contract as stipulated in the Conditions of Contract and the Appendix hereto.

Unless and until a formal Agreement is prepared and executed this Tender together with your written acceptance thereof, shall constitute a binding Contract between us.

We understand that you are not bound to accept the lowest or any tender you may receive.

We are, Gentlemen.

Yours faithfully,

Signature ....

Address ....

....……

Date ....

* Complete as appropriate

FORM OF TENDER (APPENDIX)

(NOTE: Relevant Clause numbers are shown in brackets)

Appendix - Part 1 (to be completed prior to the invitation to tender)

1   Name of the Employer (Clause 1(1)(a)) ....…...…......

    Address ....…….

2   Name of the Engineer (Clause 1(1)(c)) ....

    Address...............................……...

3   Defects Correction Period (Clause 1(1)(s))   ....weeks

4   Parts or Sections of the Works which shall not be sub-contracted without the Engineer's prior written approval (Clause 4(2))

    ....

    ....

    ....

5   Number and type of copies of Drawings to be provided (Clause 6(1)(b)) ....….

    ....

6   Form of Agreement (Clause 9)   Required/Not required

7   Performance Bond (Clause 10(1))   Required/Not required

    Amount of Bond (if required) to be   ....% of Tender Total

8   Minimum amount of third party insurance (persons and property) (Clause 23(3))   £ ....
    for each and every occurrence

9   Works Commencement Date (if known) (Clause 41(1)(a)) ....

10 Time for Completion (Clause 43) [a]

    EITHER for the whole of the Works   ....weeks

    OR for Sections of the Works (Clause 1(1)(u)) [b]

        Section A ....weeks

        Section B ....weeks

        Section C ....weeks

        Section D ....weeks

        the Remainder of the Works   ....weeks

11 Liquidated damages for delay (Clause 47)

	per day/week	limit of liability [c]
EITHER for the whole of the Works	£..............................	£...............................
OR for Section A (as above)	£..............................	£...............................
Section B (as above)	£..............................	£...............................
Section C (as above)	£..............................	£...............................
Section D (as above)	£..............................	£...............................
the Remainder of the Works (as above)	£..............................	£...............................

12 Vesting of materials not on Site (Clauses 54(4) and 60(1)(c)) (if required by the Employer) [d]

1..   4.….................................

2..   5....................................

3.............................…..   6...................................

13 Method of measurement adopted in preparation of Bills of Quantities (Clause 57) [e]...............................

....

14 Percentage of the value of goods and materials to be included

in Interim Certificates (Clause 60(2)(b))   ....%

15 Minimum amount of Interim Certificates (Clause 60(3))   £...............

16 Rate of retention (recommended not to exceed 5%) (Clause 60(5))   ....%

17 Limit of retention (% of Tender Total) (Clause 60(5)) (Recommended not to exceed 3%)   ....%

18 Bank whose Base Lending Rate is to be used (Clause 60(7)) ....….

19 Requirement for prior approval by the Employer before the Engineer can act.
DETAILS TO BE GIVEN AND CLAUSE NUMBER STATED (Clause 2(1)(b)) [f]

....

....

....

20 Name of the Planning Supervisor (Clause 71(1)(b))

....

Address ....

21 Name of the Principal Contractor (if appointed) (Clause 71(1)(b))

....

Address ....…...….......

22   The arbitration procedure to be used is (Clause 66(11)(a)

(a)   The Institution of Civil Engineers' Arbitration Procedure 1997 [g]

(b)   The Construction Industry Model Arbitration Rules [g]

---

[a]   If not stated is to be completed by Contractor in Part 2 of the Appendix.

[b]   To be completed if required, with brief description. Where Sectional completion applies the item for "the Remainder of the Works" must be used to cover the balance of the Works if the Sections described do not in total comprise the whole of the Works.

[c]   Delete where not required.

[d]   (If used) Materials to which the Clauses apply must be listed in Part I (Employer's option) or Part 2 (Contractor's option)

[e]   Insert here any amendment or modification adopted if different from that stated in Clause 57.

[f]   If there is any requirement that the Engineer has to obtain prior approval from the Employer before he can act full particulars of such requirements must be set out above.

[g]   Delete one as appropriate.

Appendix - Part 2

(To be completed by Contractor)

1   Insurance Policy Excesses (Clause 25(2))

Insurance of the Works (Clause 21(1))   £.....................

Third party (property damage) (Clause 23(1))   £.....................

2   Time for Completion (Clause 43) (if not completed in Part I of the Appendix)

EITHER for the whole of the Works   ....weeks

OR for Sections of the Works (Clause l(1)(u)) (as detailed in Part 1 of the Appendix)

Section A ....weeks

Section B ....weeks

Section C ....weeks

Section D ....weeks

the Remainder of the Works   ....weeks

3   Vesting of materials not on site (Clauses 54(4) and 60(1)(c)) (at the option of the Contractor — see [d] in Part 1)

1 ....   4 ....

2 ....   5 ....

3 ....   6 ....

4   Percentage(s) for adjustment of PC sums (Clauses 59(2)(c) and 59(5)(c)) (with details if required)

....

....

Form of Agreement

THIS AGREEMENT made the .... day of .... 19 ....

BETWEEN ....

of...

in the County of ....(hereinafter called "the Employer")

and ....

of ....

in the County of..(hereinafter called "the Contractor").

WHEREAS the Employer is desirous that certain Works should be constructed, namely the Permanent

and Temporary Works in connection with..

....

and has accepted a Tender by the Contractor for the construction and completion of such Works.

NOW THIS AGREEMENT WITNESSETH as follows

1.   In this Agreement words and expressions shall have the same meanings as are respectively assigned to them in the Conditions of Contract hereinafter referred to.

2.   The following documents shall be deemed to form and be read and construed as part of this Agreement, namely

        (a) the said Tender and the written acceptance thereof
        (b) the Drawings
        (c) the Conditions of Contract
        (d) the Specification
        (e) the priced Bill of Quantities.

3.   In consideration of the payments to be made by the Employer to the Contractor as hereinafter mentioned the Contractor hereby covenants with the Employer to construct and complete the Works in conformity in all respects with the provisions of the Contract.

4.   The Employer hereby covenants to pay to the Contractor in consideration of the construction and completion of the Works the Contract Price at the times and in the manner prescribed by the Contract.

IN WITNESS whereof the parties hereto have caused this Agreement to be executed the day and year first above written.

SIGNED on behalf of the said ....Ltd/plc (the Employer)

Signature ....   Signature ....

Position ....   Position ....

In the presence of ....   In the presence of ....

SIGNED on behalf of the said ....Ltd/plc (the Contractor)

Signature ....   Signature ....

Position ....   Position ....

In the presence of ....   In the presence of ....

or

SIGNED [and SEALED*] AS A DEED by the said   ....

....Ltd/plc (the Employer)

In the presence of ....

or

SIGNED [and SEALED*] AS A DEED by the said   ....

....Ltd/plc (the Contractor)

In the presence of ....

* Delete as appropriate

ICE FORM OF DEFAULT BOND

Date

Parties

[Names addresses and Company Numbers if applicable]

SURETY (1)

CONTRACTOR (2)

EMPLOYER (3)

Background

(A)   By a Contract defined in the Schedule hereto the Contractor has agreed with the Employer to construct and complete the Works.

(B)   The Surety has agreed to provide this Bond in favour of the Employer in order to guarantee the performance by the Contractor of his obligations under the Contract.

Surety's obligation   1

(1)   If the Contractor fails to pay the Excess Sum within 28 days of receipt by the Contractor of a copy of a certificate issued by the Engineer under clause 65(5) of the Contract the Surety hereby guarantees to the Employer that the Surety shall subject to the terms and conditions of this Bond pay the Excess Sum in accordance with Clause 1(3) up to the Bond Amount.

(2)   It shall be a condition precedent to payment by the Surety that the Employer serve on the Surety a copy of the certificate issued by the Engineer under clause 65(5) of the Contract as served on the Contractor and certified by the Engineer as being a true copy of such certificate.

(3)   Subject to Clause 1(4) payment by the Surety shall be made not later than 14 days after the later of

(a)   the expiry of the 28 day period referred to in Clause 1(1) (save in respect of any payment made by the Contractor within that time) and

(b)   service on the Surety of the copy certificate referred to in Clause 1(2).

(4)   If the Surety objects to the contents of or entitlement to issue a certificate under clause 65(5) of the Contract in respect of which the Employer seeks payment from him the Surety shall have the right to refer the matter to adjudication in accordance with the adjudication provisions contained in sub-clauses 66(6) to 66(8) of the Contract as if the Surety were a party to the Contract in place of the Contractor.

(5)   Any adjudication under Clause 1(4) shall be commenced by the Surety within 14 days of receipt by the Surety of the documents referred to in Clause 1(2) and the Surety shall have no right to refer the matter to adjudication after that time.

(6)   If the content of or entitlement to issue the Certificate under clause 65(5) of the Contract in respect of which payment is sought by the Employer is or has been the subject of an adjudication between the Employer and Contractor under the Contract (in respect of which both parties have made submissions to the adjudicator) the Surety agrees to be bound by the result of such adjudication and shall have no right to refer the matter to adjudication under Clause 1(4).

(7)   In the case of an adjudication under Clause 1(4) payment by the Surety shall be made within 7 days of the decision in such adjudication.

Surety's rights   2   (1)   The Surety shall be entitled to receive copies of any notice given by the Employer under clause 65(1) of the Contract (with any Engineer's certificate referred to) within 7 days of such notice or certificate being served on the Contractor.

(2)   The Surety shall be entitled at any time within 7 days of receipt by the Surety of the copy certificate referred to in Clause 1(2)

(a)   to request the Employer to provide the Surety with such further information and documentation as the Surety may reasonably require to verify the Excess Sum (including information or documentation held by the Engineer) and/or

(b)   to request to inspect the Site and the Works upon reasonable notice (the Employer may require that a representative of the Employer accompanies the Surety during such inspections).

Accounting   3   (1)   If the Excess Sum is subsequently determined by reason of a subsequent certificate issued by the Engineer under clause 65(5) of the Contract or by adjudication arbitration litigation or agreement between the Surety and the Employer to be less than the amount paid by the Surety the difference (if the Excess Sum has already been paid by the Surety) shall be repaid by the Employer to the Surety with Interest within 14 days (or such other period as the adjudicator arbitrator or Court may direct) after the date of such determination or agreement.

(2)   If the Excess Sum is subsequently determined or agreed to be greater than the amount already paid by the Surety any difference (up to the Bond Amount) shall be paid by the Surety to the Employer within 14 days (or such other period as the adjudicator arbitrator or Court may direct) after the date of such determination or agreement.

Interest   4   Subject to the amount payable by the Surety being varied in accordance with Clause 3 above in the event that any amount payable by either the Surety or the Employer under this Bond is not made by the date determined by Clause 1(3) or in accordance with Clause 3 (the Due Date) then the payer shall pay Interest on the sum from the Due Date until the date of payment.

Expiry 5 Save in respect of any failure to pay the Excess Sum in respect of which a claim in writing has been received beforehand from the Employer by the Surety this Bond shall expire on the earlier of the date stated in a certificate of substantial completion issued by the Engineer and the Final Expiry Date.

Forbearance 6 The Surety shall not be discharged or released by any alteration variation or waiver of any of the terms and conditions and provisions of the Contract or in any extent or nature of the Works and no allowance of time by the Employer under or in connection with the Contract or the Works shall in any way release reduce or affect the liability of the Surety under this Bond.

Governing law 7 This Bond shall be governed and construed in accordance with the laws of the country named in the Schedule ("the Country") and the courts of the Country shall have exclusive jurisdiction.

Assignment 8 This Bond may only be assigned by the Employer with the prior consent of the Surety and the Contractor which consent shall not be unreasonably withheld. In the event of any such assignment the Employer and assignee shall remain jointly and severally liable for any repayment due to the Surety under Clause 3(1). Notice of any assignment shall be given to the Surety as soon as practicable.

EXECUTED AS A DEED

on behalf of the Surety (1) director _____

(2) director/secretary _____

on behalf of the Contractor (1) director _____

(2) director/secretary _____

on behalf of the Employer (1) director _____

(2) director/secretary _____

SCHEDULE

Address for Service

Contractor:

Tel: Fax:

Employer:

Tel: Fax:

Surety:

Tel: Fax:

"Bond Amount"   means the sum of £[   ] ([   ] pounds)
                       being the maximum aggregate liability of the Surety under this Bond.

"Contract"   means the contract [made between the Employer and the Contractor dated the

                       [   ] day of [   ] [   ]] / [to be entered into between the

                        Employer and the Contractor] incorporating the ICE Conditions of Contract 7th
                        Edition.

"Excess Sum"   an amount certified as due to the Employer under Clause 65(5) of the Contract.

"Engineer" "Works" and   have the same meaning as in the Contract.
"Site"

"Final Expiry Date"   means the [   ] day of [   ] [   ].

"Interest"   means the rate of interest specified in the Contract.

"The Country"   means [England and Wales] [Scotland] [Northern Ireland]

(This Bond has been drafted in collaboration with S. J. BERWIN & Co)

The Institution of   The Association of   The Civil Engineering
Civil Engineers   Consulting Engineers   Contractors Association

This clause has been prepared by The Institution of Civil Engineers, The Association of Consulting Engineers and The Civil Engineering Contractors Association, in consultation with the Government in its revised form, for use in appropriate cases as a Special Condition of the Conditions of Contract for use in connection with the ICE Conditions of Contract SEVENTH EDITION dated September 1999.

CONTRACT PRICE FLUCTUATIONS
CIVIL ENGINEERING WORK

(1)   The amount payable by the Employer to the Contractor upon the issue by the Engineer of an interim certificate pursuant to Clause 60(2) or of the final certificate pursuant to Clause 60(4) (other than amounts due under this Clause) shall be increased or decreased in accordance with the provisions of this Clause if there shall be any changes in the following Index Figures compiled by the Department of the Environment Transport and the Regions and published by The Stationery Office in the Monthly Bulletin of Indices "1990 Series Civil Engineering Formula Indices" and "1990 Series Structural Steelwork Formula Indices"

        (a)   the Index of Labour and Supervision (Index 1)

        (b)   the Index of providing and maintaining Contractor's Equipment (Index 2 - Plant and Road Vehicles)

        (c)   the Indices of material prices applicable to those materials listed in sub-clause (4) of this Clause.

The net total of such increases and decreases shall be given effect to in determining the Contract Price.

(2)   For the purpose of this Clause

        (a)   'Final Index Figure' shall mean any Index Figure appropriate to sub-clause (1) of this Clause not qualified in the said bulletin as provisional

        (b)   'Base Index Figure' shall mean the appropriate Final Index Figure applicable to the date 42 days prior to the date for the return of tenders

        (c)   'Current Index Figure' shall mean the appropriate Final Index Figure to be applied in respect of any certificate issued or due to be issued by the Engineer pursuant to Clause 60 and shall be the appropriate Final Index Figure applicable to the date 42 days prior to

            (i)   the due date (or extended date) for completion or

            (ii)   the date certified pursuant to Clause 48 of completion of the whole of the Works or

            (iii)   the last day of the period to which the certificate relates

whichever is the earliest.

Provided that in respect of any work the value of which is included in any such certificate and which work forms part of a Section for which the due date (or extended date) for completion or the date certified pursuant to Clause 48 of completion of such Section precedes the last day of the period to which the certificate relates the Current Index Figure shall be the Final Index Figure applicable to the date 42 days prior to whichever of these dates is the earliest.

(d)   The 'Effective Value' in respect of the whole or any Section of the Works shall be the difference between

(i)   the amount which in the opinion of the Engineer is due to the Contractor under Clause 60(2) (before deducting retention) or the amount due to the Contractor under Clause 60(4) (but in each case before deducting sums previously paid on account) less any amounts for Dayworks Nominated Sub-contractors or any other items based on actual cost or current prices and any sums for increases or decreases in the Contract Price under this Clause and

(ii)   the amount calculated in accordance with (i) above and included in the last preceding interim certificate issued by the Engineer in accordance with Clause 60.

Provided that in the case of the first certificate the Effective Value shall be the amount calculated in accordance with sub-paragraph (i) above.

(3)   The increase or decrease in the amounts otherwise payable under Clause 60 pursuant to sub-clause (1) of this Clause shall be calculated by multiplying the Effective Value by a Price Fluctuation Factor which shall be the net sum of the products obtained by multiplying each of the proportions given in (a) (b) and (c) of sub-clause (4) of this Clause by a fraction the numerator of which is the relevant Current Index Figure minus the relevant Base Index Figure and the denominator of which is the relevant Base Index Figure.

(4)   For the purpose of calculating the Price Fluctuation Factor the proportions referred to in sub-clause (3) of this Clause shall (irrespective of the actual constituents of the work) be as follows and the total of such proportions shall amount to unity

(a)   0.____ *   in respect of labour and supervision costs subject to adjustment by reference to the Index referred to in sub-clause (1)(a) of this Clause. (Index 1)

(b)   0.____ *   in respect of costs of provision and use of Contractor's Equipment which shall be subject to adjustment by reference to the Index referred to in sub-clause (1)(b) of this Clause. (Index 2)

(c)   the following proportions in respect of the materials named which shall be subject to adjustment by reference to the relevant indices referred to in sub-clause (1)(c) of this Clause

0.___ *	in respect of Aggregates. (Index 3)
0.___ *	in respect of Bricks and Clay Products. (Index 4)
0.___ *	in respect of Cements. (Index 5)
0.___ *	in respect of Ready Mixed Concrete. (Index 6)
0.___ *	in respect of Cast and Spun Iron Products. (Index 7)
0.___ *	in respect of Plastics Products. (Index 8)
0.___ *	in respect of Coated Macadam and Bituminous Products. (Index 9)
0.___ *	in respect of Fuel for plant to which the DERV Fuel Index will be applied. (Index 10)
0.___ *	in respect of Fuel for plant to which the Gas Oil Fuel Index will be applied. (Index 11)
0.___ *	in respect of Timber. (Index 12)
0.___ *	in respect of Steel for Reinforcement. (Index 13)
0.___ *	in respect of Metal Sections. (Index 14)
0.___ *	in respect of Sheet Steel Piling. (Index 15)
0.___ *	in respect of Structural Steelwork Materials for Civil Engineering Works (Index S3)

(d)   0. 10   in respect of all other costs which shall not be subject to any adjustment

Total   1.00

(5)   Provisional Index Figures in the Bulletin referred to in sub-clause (1) of this Clause may be used for the provisional adjustment of interim valuations but such adjustments shall be subsequently recalculated on the basis of the corresponding Final Index Figures.

(6)   Clause 69 – Tax Fluctuations – shall not apply except to the extent that any matter dealt with therein is not covered by the Index of the Cost of Labour in Civil Engineering Construction.

*   To be filled in by the Employer prior to inviting tenders.

The Institution of   The Association of   The Civil Engineering
Civil Engineers   Consulting Engineers   Contractors Association

This clause has been prepared by The Institution of Civil Engineers, The Association of Consulting Engineers and The Civil Engineering Contractors Association, in consultation with the Government in its revised form, for use in appropriate cases as a Special Condition of the Conditions of Contract for use in connection with the ICE Conditions of Contract SEVENTH EDITION dated September 1999.

CONTRACT PRICE FLUCTUATIONS STRUCTURAL STEELWORK

(1)   The amount payable by the Employer to the Contractor upon the issue by the Engineer of an interim certificate pursuant to Clause 60(2) or of the final certificate pursuant to Clause 60(4) (other than amounts due under this Clause) shall be increased or decreased in accordance with the provisions of this Clause if there shall be any changes in the following Index Figures compiled by the Department of the Environment Transport and the Regions and published by the Stationery Office in the Monthly Bulletin of Indices "1990 Series Structural Steelwork Formula Indices"

(a)   the Index of Labour in fabrication of Structural Steelwork and erection of Structural Steelwork (Index S1)

(b)   the Index for Structural Steelwork Materials (Civil Engineering Works) (Index S3).

The net total of such increases and decreases shall be given effect to in determining the Contract Price.

(2)   For the purpose of this Clause

(a)   'Structural Steelwork' shall mean those items of work listed in sub-clause (6) of this Clause and shall include any variations as may be ordered under Clause 51 involving work of a description which in the opinion of the Engineer is similar to the description of the items so listed

(b)   'Final Index Figure' shall mean any Index Figure appropriate to sub-clause (1) of this Clause not qualified in the said bulletin as provisional

(c)   'Base Index Figure' shall mean the appropriate Final Index Figure applicable to the date 42 days prior to the date for the return of tenders

(d)   'Current Index Figure' shall mean the appropriate Final Index Figure to be applied in respect of any certificate issued or due to be issued by the Engineer pursuant to Clause 60 being such figure applicable

(i)   in respect of labour employed in fabrication - to a date 56 days prior to the last day of the period to which the certificate relates or

(ii)   in respect of labour employed in erection - to a date 14 days prior to the last day of the period to which the certificate relates or

(iii)   in respect of materials specifically purchased for inclusion in the Works - to the date of delivery to the fabricator's premises (of which date the Contractor shall produce such evidence relating to gross tonnages delivered as the Engineer may reasonably require) or

(iv)   in respect of materials (if any) not specifically purchased for inclusion in the Works – to the date of the last of the deliveries referred to in sub-paragraph (iii) of this paragraph

as the case may be.

Provided always that should the due date (or extended date) for completion or the date certified pursuant to Clause 48 of completion of the whole of the Works precede any of the aforesaid then such due date or extended date or certified date whichever is earliest shall be substituted for those aforesaid.

Provided further that if in respect of any work which forms part of a Section and whose value is included in any certificate the due date (or extended date) for completion of that Section or the date certified pursuant to Clause 48 of completion of that Section precede any of the dates aforesaid in sub-paragraphs (i) to (iv) above then such due date or extended date or certified date whichever is the earliest in respect of that Section shall be substituted for those aforesaid.

(e)   The 'Effective Value' in respect of the whole or any Section of the Works shall be the difference between

(i)   the amount which in the opinion of the Engineer is due to the Contractor under Clause 60(2) (before deducting retention) or the amount due to the Contractor under Clause 60(4) (but in each case before deducting sums previously paid on account) less any amounts for Dayworks Nominated Sub-contractors or any other items based on actual cost or current prices and any sums for increases or decreases in the Contract Price under this Clause and

(ii)   the amount calculated in accordance with (i) above and included in the last preceding interim certificate issued by the Engineer in accordance with Clause 60.

Provided that in the case of the first certificate the Effective Value shall be the amount calculated in accordance with sub-paragraph (i) above.

(3)   The Effective Value shall be apportioned between labour and materials in the following manner that is to say

(a)   labour

(i)   employed in erection - by multiplying the total tonnage erected during the period to which the certificate relates by the average cost per tonne entered at (b) of sub-clause (5) of this Clause

(ii)   employed in fabrication and delivery - by deducting the summation of the values calculated in respect of materials and in respect of labour employed in erection from the Effective Value

(b)   materials

by multiplying the total tonnage of steel delivered to the Site for inclusion in the Works during the period to which the certificate relates by the average price per tonne entered at (a) of sub-clause (5) of this Clause.

(4) (a) The increase or decrease in the amounts otherwise payable under Clause 60 pursuant to sub-clause (1) of this Clause shall be calculated by multiplying each portion of the Effective Value by a fraction the numerator of which is the product of 0.90 and the difference between the relevant Current Index Figure and the relevant Base Index Figure and the denominator of which is the relevant Base Index Figure.

(b) The relevant indices to be used in connection with this sub-clause are

(i) for labour in fabrication and erection-the Index referred to in sub-clause (1)(a) of this Clause (Index S1)

(ii) for materials – the Index referred to in sub-clause (1)(b) of this Clause (Index S3).

(5) For the purpose of the apportionment in sub-clause (3) of this Clause the full average costs per tonne (inclusive of all associated labour plant power maintenance overheads and profit) to be used are

(a) Materials delivered to fabricators premises   £   per tonne *

(b) Erection   £   per tonne *

(c) Subject to sub-paragraphs (i) (ii) and (iii) of this paragraph the relevant figures to be used in connection with this sub-clause shall be in accordance with sub-clause (2) of this Clause.

Provided that in respect of materials

(i) the Current Index Figure subsequent to the first established Current Index Figure pursuant to sub-clause (2) (d) (iii) of this Clause shall not be used until a tonnage of steel greater than the tonnage to which the Current Index Figure first established applies has been delivered to the Site for inclusion in the Works and

(ii) for the purpose of establishing the appropriate subsequent Current Index Figures to apply to all later deliveries of steel to the Site for inclusion in the Works the provisions of sub-paragraph (i) of this paragraph shall apply mutatis mutandis and

(iii) the Current Index Figure referred to in sub-clause (2) (d) (iv) of this Clause shall not be used until the total tonnage of steel delivered to the Site for inclusion in the Works exceeds the total tonnage of steel specifically purchased for inclusion in the Works and delivered to the fabricator's premises.

(6) For the purposes of this Clause the expression 'Structural Steelwork' shall comprise only those items listed hereunder †

Bill No †	Page No †	Item No †

(7)   Provisional Index Figures in the Bulletin referred to in sub-clause (1) of this Clause may be used for the provisional adjustment of interim valuations but such adjustments shall be subsequently recalculated on the basis of the corresponding Final Index Figures.

(8)   Clause 69 – Tax Fluctuations – shall not apply except to the extent that any matter dealt with therein is not covered by the Index of the Cost of Labour in fabrication of steelwork and erection of steelwork.

*   To be filled in by the Contractor at the time of tendering.

†   To be filled in by the Employer prior to inviting tenders.

| The Institution of | The Association of | The Civil Engineering |
| Civil Engineers | Consulting Engineers | Contractors Association |

This clause has been prepared by The Institution of Civil Engineers, The Association of Consulting Engineers and The Civil Engineering Contractors Association, in consultation with the Government in its revised form, for use in appropriate cases as a Special Condition of the Conditions of Contract for use in connection with the ICE Conditions of Contract SEVENTH EDITION dated September 1999.

CONTRACT PRICE FLUCTUATIONS
CIVIL ENGINEERING WORK AND STRUCTURAL STEELWORK

(1)   This Clause shall apply only to those contracts which incorporate the Contract Price Fluctuation Clause Revised February 1999 for Civil Engineering work and the Structural Steelwork Clause Revised February 1999 (referred to in this Clause as the CEW Clause and the SS Clause respectively).

(2)   For the purposes of this Clause

        (a)   'Civil Engineering work' shall mean all Works with the exception of Structural Steelwork and

        (b)   ' Structural Steelwork' shall mean the work defined in sub-clause (2)(a) of the SS Clause.

(3)   The Effective Value (as defined both in the CEW Clause and in the SS Clause) shall be sub-divided to show the amounts included in respect of the Civil Engineering work and the Structural Steelwork. The amount in respect of the former shall then be treated as if it were the Effective Value as defined in the CE Clause and adjusted in accordance with the provisions of that Clause. The amount in respect of the latter shall then be treated as if it were the Effective Value as defined in the SS Clause and adjusted in accordance with that Clause.